OH

Off the Beaten Path

"Over a two-year period, Zimmermann visited all 88 Ohio counties, searching out interesting inns, restaurants, historic sites, scenic spots and unusual stores. ... Nostalgia, tranquility and charm are predominant characteristics of the sites—antidotes to fast-paced city life."
—*Cincinnati Post*

"Offers a different peek at our state from its back roads and byways ... includes restored canal towns and gristmills, forests, elegant and casual dining establishments and overnight accommodations."
—The *Columbus Dispatch*

"There are separate sections in the book on all the different counties in Ohio, establishing clearly that the Buckeye State has a wide variety of attractions."
—Erie, Pennsylvania, *Times-News*

"Focuses on the lesser-known attractions of the Buckeye State—picturesque Amish villages, an Ohio River town that served as a station on the Underground Railroad, local wineries, clusters of antique shops, and a general store that stocks everything from fresh buffalo meat to tomahawks."
—Lexington (KY) *Herald-Leader*

"Explores a surprising number of 'undiscovered' treasures—and some discovered ones as well."
—The *Blade*, Toledo, OH

"Zimmermann complimented the Ohio Historical Society for having more good sites than many other areas in the country."
—The *Columbus Citizen-Journal*

OHIO

Off the Beaten Path

Third Edition

by **George Zimmermann**

ILLUSTRATED BY
Keith Knore

A Voyager Book

Chester, Connecticut

Copyright © 1983, 1985, 1988 by George Zimmermann

All rights reserved. No part of this book may be reproduced without permission from the publisher, except by a reviewer who may quote brief passages in a review; nor may any part of this book be reproduced, stored in a retrieval system or transmitted in any form or by any means, electronic, mechanical, photocopying, recording or other, without permission from the publisher. Requests for permission should be made in writing to The Globe Pequot Press, 138 West Main Street, Chester CT 06412.

Library of Congress Cataloging-in-Publication Data

Zimmermann, George, 1952–
  Ohio, off the beaten path.

  Includes index.
  1. Ohio—Description and travel—1981—Guide—
books. I. Title.
F489.3.Z55 1988   917.71'0443   84-4308
ISBN 0-87106-740-4

Cover design by Barbara Marks
Cover illustration of Buckeye Furnace by Keith Knore
Typography by TRG

Manufactured in the United States of America
Third Edition / Third Printing

*To
Susan
and
Brian*

Ohio

Northwest

Northeast

West Central

East Central

Southwest

Southeast

Contents

About the Author

George Zimmermann reports on Ohio state government and politics as the Manager of Television Services/Administrator for the Ohio Public Radio/Public Television Statehouse Bureau. He has worked in broadcasting for the past fifteen years, primarily writing, producing, directing and reporting for public television stations in Texas and Ohio. He spent a year in Los Angeles editing situation comedies, including "The Jeffersons."

An inveterate traveler, Zimmermann was prompted to write this guide when he moved to Ohio in 1979 and wanted information about Ohio's attractions. He spent two years roaming Ohio's backroads and researching the points of interest included in this guide. Zimmermann lives in Columbus with his son Brian.

About the Illustrator

Keith Knore is the creative director for Slidemasters, a Columbus, Ohio, computer graphics firm. Previously, he worked as a television graphic design artist. In 1976 he won two Emmy awards for scenic design and title graphics from the Columbus-Dayton-Cincinnati Chapter of the National Academy of Television Arts and Sciences.

Acknowledgments

My thanks to the Ohio Department of Natural Resources, the Ohio Office of Travel, and Tourism and the Ohio Historical Society, Inc. for providing supplemental information and materials about many of the places described in this book. Their cooperation made researching *Ohio: Off the Beaten Path* a productive and enjoyable endeavor.

Introduction

Ohio is an excellent state to explore—it has breathtaking natural beauty a rich historical heritage, countless fine restaurants, and varied and unique overnight lodging. *Ohio: Off the Beaten Path* exposes the reader to Ohio's best—from rolling pastoral farmland to rugged wooded cliffs and gorges, from restored canal towns and gristmills to country inns and working historical farms. After years of researching and traveling the state, I can only conclude that Ohio offers a wealth of opportunities for recreation, for appreciating the history that shaped its present and future, and for pleasurable excursions to suit any tastes or interests.

Most of the destinations described in this book, be they historical, culinary, or recreational, are located away from interstate highways and major metropolitan areas—an indication of my own preference for scenic roads and picturesque towns and villages (traveling by interstate highway just does not provide the enjoyment of winding through forests and cresting hills on a narrow, two-lane country road). For this reason, to take full advantage of *Ohio: Off the Beaten Path*, you will need an Ohio highway map. The Ohio Office of Travel and Tourism will mail you a map at no charge if you call (toll-free) 1-800-BUCKEYE or write to P.O. Box 1001, Columbus, Ohio 43216. That toll-free number can also provide another valuable service—confirmation of specific information on thousands of sites and attractions around the state. While every effort has been made to insure that addresses, phone numbers, rates, hours, and seasons of the places described in this book are accurate at the time of publication, establishments do change owners or hours of operation, relocate, and even close. For this reason, I advise taking advantage of the state's toll-free service to verify important information before making that two- or three-hour drive.

Because of frequent changes in menu selections and prices, restaurant prices in this book are given by category:

inexpensive - less than $6

moderate - $6 to $10

expensive - more than $10

These price ranges reflect the cost of entrees and do not include beverages, desserts, tips, or tax.

Whether spending a week, a weekend, or just an afternoon traveling to a new destination, you will probably find as I did that Ohio's friendly people and splendid countryside make any trip that much more rewarding. And if you have yet to experience the state's historic and recreational opportunities, I believe you will be impressed and amazed by all Ohio has to offer.

Off the Beaten Path in Northeast Ohio

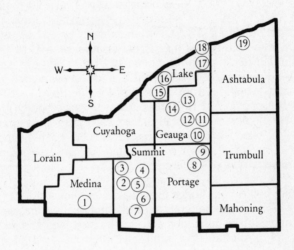

1. Oaks Lodge
2. Hale Farm and Western Reserve Village
3. The Taverne of Richfield
4. Blossom Music Center
5. Stan Hywet Hall
6. Perkins Mansion/John Brown Home
7. Portage House
8. Hopkins Old Water Mill
9. Nelson Kennedy Ledges State Park/Nelson Ledges Quarry Park
10. Welshfield Inn
11. Middlefield Cheese House
12. Burton Sugar Camp/Century Village
13. Richards Maple Products/Cleveland Soaring Society
14. Inn at Fowler's Mill
15. Holden Arboretum
16. Lawnfield
17. Chalet Debonne Vineyards/Grand River Vineyard
18. Old Tavern
19. Ashtabula Harbor/Hulbert's Restaurant

Northeast Ohio

Medina County

Tranquil, stream-fed Chippewa Lake provides the setting for an outstanding country dining establishment, the **Oaks Lodge**. Eight acres of tall trees surround this rambling former estate, which rests a stone's throw from the water. Railroad industrialist J. F. Townsend remodeled this former farmhouse in 1914, using it to entertain such captains of industry as J. Pierpont Morgan. Townsend dubbed the place Five Oaks for the semicircle of oak trees that graced the front of the home at the time.

Don Casper and Al Hitchins purchased the property in 1961 and, over the past three decades, have earned a reputation for an innovative menu and an impressive kitchen. Each of the four dining areas has its own distinct character, and the large windows allow a view of the large patio—a perfect spot for a cocktail or after-dinner drink—and the gazebo at water's edge.

Dinner at the Oaks Lodge includes dishes such as rack of lamb, roast prime rib, several cuts of steak, and veal gesina, which is veal sauteed in wine, butter, and mushrooms. Seafood fans can choose from Alaskan king crab legs, fresh trout, shrimp tempura, and the broiled shore dinner—a combination of lobster, scampi, haddock, tomatoes, mushrooms, peppers, and onions served on a skewer. A favorite with many regulars here is the broiled scampi in parsley and garlic butter served in individual chafing dishes.

A fine dinner salad distinguishes a quality restaurant from an ordinary one, and an Oaks Lodge salad comes brimming with fresh scallions, carrots, salad peppers, and tomatoes. For your choice of potato, try the unusual potatoes anna—pan-fried spuds smothered in onions and peppers. The lodge's luxurious desserts include grand marnier chocolate mousse, chocolate cheesecake, and an assortment of parfaits. From the fresh flowers and stylish decor (the lodge has won several awards for interior design) to the culinary expertise, the Oaks Lodge rates high marks.

The Oaks Lodge is on Medina County Road #19. On the Lake at Chippewa; (216) 769-2601. Open Tuesday through Friday, 11:30 A.M.–2:30 P.M.; Tuesday through Thursday, 5–10 P.M.; Friday and Saturday, 5–11 P.M.; Sunday, 11 A.M.–8 P.M. Prices: moderate to expensive. MasterCard, Visa, and American Express are accepted. Reservations recommended.

Medina County is also the location of a unique annual occurrence—Ohio's equivalent of the swallows returning to Capistrano. Each year on March 15, seventy-five turkey vultures come home to roost in trees by the cliffs and caverns of **Whipp's Ledges** near Hinckley. With clocklike regularity, the buzzards have returned to this summer home for the past 150 years. Hinckley townspeople mark the occasion with celebrations on the first Sunday after March 15, when a "buzzard breakfast" is served.

Summit County

The Western Reserve region of Ohio was "reserved" for settlers moving west from Connecticut after the American Revolution. One of those settlers, Jonathan Hale, relocated his family in 1810, establishing a farm in the rolling acreage of what is today northern Summit County. The Hale property remained in the family until the death of Miss Clara Belle Ritchie, great-granddaughter of Jonathan, in 1956. She willed the farm to the Western Reserve Historical Society, stipulating that it be opened to the public so that as many people as possible could "be informed as to the history and culture of the Western Reserve."

The history and culture of the region are faithfully preserved at the working **Hale Farm and Western Reserve Village**. Costumed guides explain the significance and origins of the furnishings and artifacts displayed in the Hale farmhouse, a 150-year-old, three-story brick structure. Some of the items exhibited were transported to Ohio from Connecticut with the Hale family. The guides also demonstrate pioneer crafts and skills such as dipping candles and setting the proper tension on a rope spring bed. Behind the farmhouse, a small antique sawmill powered by a marvelous 1923 portable steam engine cuts timber into boards for use in the village.

Six buildings dating from the early 1800s make up the Western Reserve Village. United States Senator Benjamin F. Wade worked in the Law Office, built in 1820. And the large fireplace and rough-hewn floors and beams in the one-room schoolhouse typify the rustic construction techniques of the early nineteenth century. Local craftspeople demonstrate spinning and weaving in the

Stow House, and a potter, glassblower, and blacksmith work at their trades in the village. Perhaps the most intriguing building is the Meetinghouse, which was built as a Baptist church in Streetsboro, Ohio, in 1851. Sliding aside some boards behind the pulpit reveals a 4-foot-deep, 1,000-gallon tank used for total-immersion baptisms.

Hale Farm and Western Reserve Village is in the 32,000-acre Cuyahoga Valley National Recreational Area at 2686 Oak Hill Road, in Bath; (216) 666-3711 (Akron number), (216) 575-9137 (Cleveland number). Open mid-May through October, Tuesday through Saturday, 10 A.M.–5 P.M.; Sundays and holidays, noon–5 P.M. Admission: adults, $4; children (ages six–twelve) and senior citizens (ages sixty and over), $3.

The **Cuyahoga Valley National Recreation Area** follows the Cuyahoga River for twenty-two miles between Akron and Cleveland. The park offers numerous hiking, nature, and bicycle trails, scenic overlooks, and picnic areas. Winter sports in the park include sledding, ice skating, snowmobiling, and cross-country skiing. Two complete ski centers, **Brandywine**, (216) 467-8198, in Northfield, and **Boston Mills**, (216) 657-2210, in nearby Peninsula, serve downhill skiers, with complete ski shops, lifts, instruction, and equipment rentals.

If riding the train, hiking, or skiing has worked up your appetite, fine food served in a historic setting is as close as nearby Richfield. Canalboat builder and carpenter Louis B. Ellas constructed the Richfield Hotel, now called **The Taverne of Richfield**, in 1886, replacing an earlier inn destroyed by fire in 1878. The hotel provided dining, lodging in four guest rooms, and entertainment in the spacious ballroom. Ellas's nautical background is evident in the design of the second-floor ballroom—its unusual wooden ceiling resembles the inside of a ship's hull.

The Taverne no longer offers lodging, but it does serve fine food in two turn-of-the-century dining rooms. Both dining areas, the Front Parlor and the Dining Room, contain numerous antiques and period wallpapers. The Front Parlor's distinctive oak fireplace mantel dates from the 1850s, and the ten brass chandeliers originally illuminated ballrooms in Akron's old Portage Hotel. Throughout The Taverne are unusual sepia-tone glass reproductions of original glass slides taken of northern Summit County in the late nineteenth century. These are displayed in wooden frames in the windows.

Lunch at The Taverne includes a variety of salads, sandwiches, omelets, and quiche Lorraine, as well as appetizers such as sauerkraut balls, oysters on the half shell, and raw vegetables with dip.

A specialty appetizer on the dinner menu is the hot crabmeat Taverne style, which consists of Alaskan crab, green onions, mushrooms, and tomatoes in a cream sauce, topped with hollandaise and Parmesan cheese. The wide selection of dinner entrees includes imaginative dishes such as filet mignon topped with avocado slices and bearnaise sauce, apricot-glazed pork tenderloin medallions, and rack of lamb.

The wine cellar houses a raw shrimp and oyster bar during winter months, and patio dining is available in the summer. The impeccable restoration of The Taverne by executive chef Peter Girardin and owner Mel Rose has earned the structure a listing in the National Register of Historic Places.

The Taverne of Richfield is at the intersection of Rtes. 176 and 303, in Richfield; (216) 659-3155. Open for lunch Monday through Saturday, 11:30 A.M.–2:30 P.M.; for dinner Monday through Thursday, 5:30–11 P.M.; Friday and Saturday, 5:30 P.M.–midnight; and Sunday, 3:30–9 P.M. Brunch is served 10:30 A.M.–2:30 P.M. on Sunday. Prices: lunch, inexpensive to moderate; dinner, expensive. MasterCard, Visa, and American Express are accepted.

Nestled in 800 acres of rolling hills between Akron and Cleveland is one of America's premier outdoor cultural and entertainment complexes—**Blossom Music Center**. The summer home (and a major source of revenue) for the renowned Cleveland Orchestra, Blossom also attracts audiences for performances that range from opera to ballet, from jazz to rock 'n' roll.

The nation's top artists take the stage in the innovative pavilion, a fan-shaped, open-air structure seating 5,267. Its enormous roof rises 94 feet above stage level (it's the largest shingled area in the country), creating a sound chamber requiring little or no electronic amplification for those seated in the pavilion.

Four acres of lawn on the gentle hillside provide outdoor seating for another 13,000 patrons. A unique computerized sound system has a delay feature that transmits the sound from speakers at precisely the moment the sound from the stage reaches the lawn audience, creating near perfect listening conditions.

Artists perform almost every evening during the June through September season. For information and a schedule of coming attractions, call or write Blossom Music Center, 1145 West Steels Corners Road, Cuyahoga Falls, Ohio 44223. April through September, phone the center at (216) 920-1440 (Akron number) or (216) 566-9330 (Cleveland number). October through March, call (216) 231-7300.

Constructed at a cost of $2 million in 1915, Frank A. and Gertrude Seiberling's **Stan Hywet Hall** in Akron required four years to complete. Frank Seiberling founded the Goodyear and Seiberling rubber companies, and this lavish sixty-five–room mansion gives testimony to the personal wealth amassed by industrialists in that era.

Considered to be one of the finest examples of American Tudor Revival architecture, Stan Hywet is patterned after three tudor estates in England, with elements of each incorporated in the design of the structure. As is typical of Tudor buildings, windows, doors, chimneys, and roof peaks are asymmetrical and appear randomly placed. The name Stan Hywet means "stone quarry" in Anglo Saxon, a reference to the quarry once located on this 3,000-acre estate which supplied much of the stone used in the hall's construction.

Molded plaster ceilings and dark oak walls, both commonly used in English Tudor residences, can be found throughout the Seiberling home. The Seiberlings went to considerable trouble to make Stan Hywet as faithful as possible to the Tudor style—they concealed telephones behind wall coverings and installed twenty-three working fireplaces, even though the building is equipped with central heating. They also built in a rope elevator for hauling firewood from the basement to the upper floors.

Formal balls and other social functions were held in the large music room, which has three massive crystal chandeliers, sixteen wall sconces, and a second-floor balcony for a small orchestra. The formal dining room seats forty, and a mural above the oak walls depicts the story of Chaucer's *Canterbury Tales*. Rare American chestnut, a type of wood that's no longer available due to a devastating blight, lines the walls of the billiard room.

The Seiberlings removed the walls, floor, and ceiling from a room in an English manor house scheduled for demolition and installed these materials in the second-floor master bedroom. Also in their bedroom is an original Tudor canopy bed, circa 1575. Throughout the tour, guides point out many of the outstanding pieces in the Seiberling's priceless collection of antiques. The two urns in the fountain room, for example, date from before the birth of Christ.

Manicured gardens, woodlands crisscrossed with paths and trails, and splendid shrubbery surround Stan Hywet Hall. Clear stream water pours over a stone waterfall into a cool pond in the tall trees just behind the Seiberling mansion.

Stan Hywet Hall is at 714 North Portage Path, in Akron; (216) 836-5533. Open year-round (except the first two weeks in January), Tuesday through Saturday, 10 A.M.–4 P.M.; Sunday, 1–4 P.M. Admission: adults, $5; children, $2.

From Stan Hywet Hall, take Portage Path south for a drive past many fine old Akron homes and estates. If you continue south to the intersection of Copley Road and South Portage Path, you will find two museums.

The mansion of Colonel Simon Perkins was constructed adjacent to the historic Portage Path at Akron between the years 1835 and 1837. The home is an example of the Greek Revival style, which had great influence on architecture during the early settlement of the Western Reserve. Built of native sandstone on the brow of a hill, the **Perkins Mansion**, with its two-story portico, overlooks the city of Akron. Through the years, it has become recognized as one of the most imposing homes of northern Ohio.

Colonel Perkins was born to General and Mrs. Simon Perkins at Warren, Ohio, in 1805. His father organized the Western Reserve Bank in 1813, and, in connection with Paul Williams, founded the village of Akron in 1825.

Colonel Perkins, who served in the Ohio legislature and was an active promoter of the Cleveland, Zanesville & Cincinnati Railroad, purchased 115 acres of land on this site in 1832 for $1,300. Perkins and his wife, sister of the future governor of Ohio, David Tod, resided in Warren until moving to Akron in 1835. While the mansion was under construction, they lived in a small, frame house, now known as the **John Brown Home**.

Surrounded by more than ten acres of beautiful grounds, the mansion today contains some of its original furnishings, as well as items connected with the early history of Summit County. Situated on the grounds are the original carriage house, a combination summer kitchen and laundry built in 1890, the original well—dug through 40 feet of sandstone—and a garage used to exhibit antique vehicles and tools.

Across the street is the John Brown Home, so named to commemorate the two-year residency of that abolitionist leader from

7

1844 to 1846. At the time, Brown was associated with Colonel Simon Perkins in the sheep and wool business. The original frame structure, to which several additions have been made, is believed to have been built around 1830.

Both museums are operated by the Summit County Historical Society. They are open year-round except for the month of January, from Tuesday through Sunday, 1–5 P.M.; (216) 535-1120. Admission (to both museums): adults, $2; children (ages six–sixteen), $1.50.

Just up the street from the museums, Harry and Jeanne Pinnick offer bed and breakfast accommodations in their 1917 **Portage House**. Once one of Akron's most prestigious neighborhoods, today this part of town is an inner-city neighborhood that has declined through the years. But the Pinnick's three-story Tudor home provides a pleasant stop in a parklike setting for weary travelers.

Harry is a physics professor at the nearby University of Akron, and Jeanne runs the Portage House. They live on the third floor; the second-floor bedrooms are available for guests. Downstairs, the large living room is a quiet place to relax or read the evening paper.

Depending on the number of guests in the house, Jeanne serves a full breakfast either at an island in the center of the kitchen or in the formal dining room. Friendly people like the Pinnicks and modest prices are why bed and breakfast places are starting to catch on in this country (they have been popular in Europe for years). As Harry and Jeanne complete restoration of the Portage House, their incredibly reasonable rates may be increased.

The Portage House is at 601 Copley Road, Akron; (216) 535-1952. Rates: $22 to $28 per night. Personal checks accepted.

Portage County

Many visitors to Portage County are attracted by **Sea World**, a marine life park with whale and dolphin shows and other aquatic demonstrations, and **Geauga Lake**, a 240-acre amusement park with more than one hundred rides and shows, both in Aurora. However, Garrettsville has a unique point of interest far less well known—**Hopkins Old Water Mill**.

A number of Ohio gristmills provide demonstrations and infor-

Hopkins Old Water Mill

mation on the role of the miller in pioneer towns and villages, but Hopkins Old Water Mill actually performs the function it has had since 1804—grinding grains from local farms into flour and meal.

John Garrett built this water-powered mill on the banks of rushing Silver Creek. A forty-one–bucket wheel drives the grinding stones, and a system of flights (a vertical cup conveyor mechanism) transports the grain and flour to and from the various floors of the mill. Power for Hopkins Old Water Mill has not always been provided by waterwheel—in 1913 the mill was "modernized" with the installation of water turbines. The Tushar family purchased the mill in 1970, and, in 1976, reconverted it to waterwheel power.

Self-guided tours of the gristmill start at the outdoor landing, near the millrace where water is diverted from the scenic creek to turn the large wheel. French milling stones, 3,000 pounds each and quarried in 1850, grind grains into flour on the first floor. Flights convey the flour to the second floor for sifting, bagging, and storage.

The mill grinds 2,800 pounds of flour per hour. Milling takes place three times a week, but the millworks operate continuously for visitors. Members of the Tushar family gladly answer any questions about the history or operation of the mill, and fresh ground flour is sold. Hopkins Old Water Mill is one of the finest restored mills in the state.

Hopkins Old Water Mill is one block east of the intersection of Rtes. 82 and 88 at 8148 Main Street, Garrettsville; (216) 527-2705. Open Monday through Friday, 8 A.M.–6 P.M.; Saturday, 8 A.M.–4 P.M.; closed Sunday.

Nearby, a small park—**Nelson Kennedy Ledges**—rests on the precise dividing line of the region's watershed: from this spot to the east feeds the Saint Lawrence River; to the west, the Mississippi. Rugged cliffs of exposed sandstone and diverse plant life, including eastern hemlock and Canada yew, make hiking the park's five major trails both rigorous and rewarding.

A majestic 50-foot waterfall known as Cascade Falls and a narrow passageway in the rocks called Dwarfs Pass are just two of the many unusual geological formations at Nelson Kennedy Ledges. The Cayuga Indians once lived in these forests and cliffs, and Crystal Creek was the site of a mini-gold rush when iron pyrite was mistakenly identified as gold. Picnic tables and barbecue grills are provided.

Nelson Kennedy Ledges State Park is east of Parkman, 2 miles south of Rte. 422 on Rte. 282. Open daylight hours, no admission charge.

An old sand and gravel quarry turned recreation area is located just south of the state park. **Nelson Ledges Quarry Park** offers swimming and scuba diving in a spring-fed, clear-water quarry pit. Water depths range from 20 to 45 feet, and divers enjoy exploring the abandoned cars and boats at the bottom. Swimmers use the sandy beach, and the park has a separate fishing lake stocked with bass. Divers must bring their own equipment, present a national certification card (or be accompanied by an instructor), and wear a flotation vest. Visitors also may camp in the eighty-acre campground. Winter sports at Nelson Ledges include skiing and snowmobiling.

Nelson Ledges Quarry Park is on Rte. 282 east of Parkman; (216) 548-2716. Open year-round. Admission to swim or dive: Monday through Thursday, $2; Friday through Sunday, $3. Camping is $3 per night per person, plus next day's admission charge.

Geauga County

Built the 1840s by Alden J. Nash and originally called the Nash Hotel, the **Welshfield Inn** served as an Underground Railway station for slaves escaping from the South to Canada. Stagecoaches traveling between Cleveland and Pittsburgh also frequently stopped here for food and overnight accommodations.

Although lodging is no longer offered here, the tradition of serving old-fashioned country cooking has been maintained by innkeepers Brian and Pauline Holmes. The large dining room contains an eclectic mix of bentwood chairs and wooden tables; browns, greens, and other earth tones predominate, and fresh flowers dress up each table. The smaller dining room, called Peddlers Parlor, has Early American decor with antiques and blue tablecloths and drapes. On the front porch, lawn furniture creates a friendly, informal atmosphere under the tall columns. Also under the porch roof is a huge wooden sled named Snowbird capable of carrying twenty to thirty people.

Lunches at the Welshfield Inn include entrees such as chicken a la king on a biscuit, beef tenderloin tips with mushrooms on toast, French-fried scallops, and grilled ham with a pineapple slice. Fresh vegetables are served with each luncheon selection. Following the same pattern of straightforward dishes at reasonable prices, dinner entrees include broiled flounder, prime rib, baked ham with raisin sauce, and country fried chicken. Homemade desserts are a specialty at the inn, with a wide selection of fresh fruit pies and cream pies available.

The Welshfield Inn is on Rte. 422, Welshfield; (216) 834-4164. Open for lunch Tuesday through Saturday, noon–2:30 P.M.; for dinner Tuesday through Thursday, 5–8 P.M.; Friday and Saturday; 5–9 P.M.; Sunday, noon–8 P.M. Closed late December and all of January, plus July 1–15. Prices: lunch, inexpensive to moderate; dinner, moderate to expensive. MasterCard, Visa, and American Express are accepted.

Approximately 16,000 Amish live in Geauga County, making it one of the largest Amish communities in the country. Wearing the traditional dark, solid-colored clothing and rejecting modern conveniences such as electricity and automobiles, the "plain people" strive for a simple farming life. Their black, horse-drawn buggies amble down county roads, particularly near Middlefield, Ohio. Middlefield merchants provide hitching posts for their Amish customers, and the **Dutch Country Kitchen Restaurant** serves Amish-style meals in an unpretentious concrete block building.

Many of the Amish operate dairy farms, and they bring their milk to the **Middlefield Cheese House** to be manufactured into Swiss cheese. The cheese plant, founded as a cooperative in 1956 by twenty-five area farmers, is one of the largest producers of quality Swiss in the United States, with an output of more than twenty million pounds annually.

Visitors are invited to view a film, "Faith and Teamwork," which carefully describes each step in the cheese-making process. Then a tour of the Cheese House museum features Old World carvings from Switzerland, antique cheese-making equipment, Amish artifacts, and historical photos. Be sure to stop in at the Cheese Chalet Shop, where fresh sausages, homemade breads and pastries, Geauga County maple syrup, plus a wide selection of fine cheeses are available for purchase.

Middlefield Cheese House is on Rte. 608, just north of downtown Middlefield; (216) 632-5228. Open Monday through Saturday, 7:30 A.M.–5:30 P.M. No admission charge.

Mid-February through mid-April is a special time in Geauga County—maple syrup season. Those first February thaws start the sap flowing, and farmers throughout the county use special taps and buckets to drain the sap from their sugar maple trees.

Once collected, it is boiled and evaporated, with thirty to sixty gallons of sap needed to make one gallon of maple syrup. Smoke rising from area sugarhouses means syrup production is underway.

The **Burton Sugar Camp** is the only municipally owned sugar camp in the country. In a ten-acre park in the center of Burton, sap from the park's 1,500 sugar maples is boiled into syrup in a rustic log cabin. The cabin is open daily from late February through April, and maple syrup products are sold on weekends from May through the middle of December.

Across the street from the cabin is the **Maple House Bakery and Gift Shop**, which sells homemade breads, Geauga County maple syrup, honey, and preserves. A favorite here is the old-fashioned ice cream, particularly (you guessed it) the maple and maple nut flavors.

At the south end of Burton's town square is **Century Village**—fifteen restored buildings which provide a glimpse of the Western Reserve in the 1800s. The Blacksmith Shop, built in 1822, has an impressive complement of smithy tools and equipment. For a look at upper-middle-class life in the region, the Boughton House is furnished with pieces typical of the 1840s. The B&O Railroad built the Aultman station after the Civil War, and next to it sits a twenty-ton B&O caboose. Members of the Geauga County Historical Society conduct one-and-a-half-hour tours of the village.

Century Village is on the town square in Burton; (216) 834-4012, 834-4852 (country store). Open May through November, Tuesday through Saturday, 10 A.M.–5 P.M.; Sunday, 1–5 P.M. Admission: adults, $2.50; children (ages six–twelve), $1.50; senior citizens, $2.

The annual **Geauga County Maple Festival**, held on the first weekend after Easter, takes place in Chardon, 10 miles north of Burton. Parades, maple syrup contests, a quilt and afghan show, and competitions in pancake flipping and eating, wood chopping, rooster crowing, and beard shaving with an ax are just some of the activities at this yearly celebration.

The king of maple products in Geauga County has to be Paul Richards, of **Richards Maple Products**; his family has been in the business since 1910. Paul purchases tens of thousands of gallons of syrup annually from area farmers, syrup which he transforms into pure maple spread (similar to honey butter), maple sugar, maple cream (a fudgelike concoction available with or without black walnuts), maple candy, maple ice cream, and, of course, three grades of maple syrup. All of these are produced without the use of preservatives.

Richards Maple Products also sells a wide selection of gift boxes containing endless combinations of their various products. Catalogs of gift box selections are available by mail.

Richards Maple Products is at 545 Water Street (Rte. 6, west of central business district), Chardon, Ohio 44024; (216) 286-4160. Open Monday through Saturday, 9 A.M.–6 P.M.; Sunday, noon–6 P.M.

If you have ever envied an eagle or gull soaring in a gentle breeze, try a glider ride in one of the **Cleveland Soaring Society**'s two-seat gliders. The club is based near Chardon, and a trained glider pilot will let you experience the thrill of soaring from the front seat of one of the pair of trainers.

The $25 demo rides last from fifteen to thirty minutes and are offered on Wednesday afternoons and all day on weekends. No reservations are required, but since demo rides must compete with the club's sixty members for the use of the aircraft, early morning or late afternoon are probably the best times.

For those interested in pursuing the sport, membership dues, which cover all instruction and use of the society's aircraft, are $350 per year. The only additional charge for members is a $12 tow fee for use of the propellor plane which pulls the gliders aloft. The Cleveland Soaring Society is based at the Chardon Airport on Rte. 44, 2 miles south of Chardon; (216) 285-9378, 531-7901.

In the late 1960s, Jerry Micco watched his just-completed restaurant burn to the ground three days before the scheduled grand opening. While that might have deterred some, Jerry sketched a design for another restaurant while the fire department was still on the scene fighting the blaze.

A builder and designer by profession, Jerry Micco acquired a palate for fine dining through his extensive worldwide travels, and the **Inn at Fowler's Mill** reflects his interest in quality cuisine. Jerry hired Swiss master chef Stephan Reiger in 1982, and Jerry and Stephan plan to open a culinary school at Fowler's Mill. In fact, one of Jerry's sons is already studying under Stephan, while a second attends the Culinary Institute of America in New York.

Though the inn was constructed in 1970, the rustic interior

and antiques scattered throughout give the warmth of a much older structure. Four separate dining areas, each having its own character, are carefully appointed; the room featuring three glass walls is my favorite. Looking out those windows, down the hill and across the stream, one has a marvelous view of the slopes of the Alpine Valley Ski Area. Actually, the view from here is rewarding year-round, from the first buds of spring to the changing fall colors in the woodlands which surround the inn. On summer evenings, open windows allow the valley breeze to float through the dining room.

The aggressive luncheon menu includes a choice of steaks, seafood dishes such as baked filet of sole stuffed with crabmeat, grilled pork chops with stewed apples, plus a wide selection of salads, sandwiches, and omelets.

Dinner appetizers such as oysters Florentine and smoked salmon with Bermuda onions and cream cheese provide a tantalizing start to the evening meal. From there, you must choose from at least fifteen entrees offered nightly—steaks, lobster, chops, roast Long Island duck with grand marnier, rack of lamb, and chateaubriand. The nightly special might be the Inn's superb cordon bleu au gratin de champignons, with its delicately seasoned cheese and mushroom sauce. After your meal, you can stop by the friendly tavern for an after-dinner sherry or browse in the half dozen shops adjacent to the inn.

The Inn at Fowler's Mill is 4 miles east of Chesterland, at 10700 Mayfield Road (Rte. 322); (216) 729-1313. The inn is open for lunch Tuesday through Saturday, 11:30 A.M.–2:30 P.M., and for dinner Tuesday through Thursday, 5:30–10 P.M.; Friday and Saturday, 5:30–11 P.M. Prices: lunch, inexpensive to moderate; dinner, expensive. MasterCard, Visa, and American Express are accepted.

From late November to the middle of March, skiers hit the powder at the **Alpine Valley Ski Area**. This complete ski resort has six slopes and a backwoods trail, high-powered lighting towers for night skiing, and a 10,000-square-foot rental shop with 1,400 pairs of skis. Austrian Ferdl Aster runs the ski instruction program, which offers both private and group lessons. After a strenuous day on the slopes, a blazing fire in the lodge's fireplace lures skiers to it to unwind.

The Alpine Valley Ski Area is on Rte. 322, 4 miles east of Chesterland; (216) 285-2211, 729-9775 (ski reports).

Lake County

Holden Arboretum, one of the world's largest arboreta, encompasses 3,100 acres of wooded trails, ponds full of ducks and geese, fields, and deep ravines. Dedicated to increasing knowledge of the plant world, Holden has five primary nature trails which take visitors past the maple collection, renowned for its beauty when the leaves change color in the fall, the nut tree collection with its more than 150 varieties of edible nut-bearing trees, and the conifer collection of pines, firs, spruces, and junipers.

The lilac and rhododendron gardens and crabapple and shrub collections are other examples of the many and varied exhibits in this vast nature preserve. Occasional Getting-to-Know-Holden nature walks and frequent lectures are offered at the arboretum, as are memberships in the Holden Arboretum Association. Membership entitles you to free admission to the grounds, cross-country skiing privileges, and discounts on courses, lectures, and gift shop purchases. Bird watching and wildflower walks are popular at Holden, and the arboretum has special programs for children on subjects such as animal communication and summertime nature discovery sessions.

The Holden Arboretum is at 9500 Sperry Road, Mentor; (216) 946-4400. Open Tuesday through Sunday, 10 A.M.–5 P.M. Admission: adults $2.50; children (ages six–fifteen), $1.75; senior citizens, $1.75. Group rates are available. Area is wheelchair accessible.

One of Lake County's most famous residents—James Garfield—succeeded another Ohio Republican—Rutherford B. Hayes—and was elected president of the United States in 1880 and inaugurated on March 4, 1881. Assassin Charles Guiteau shot Garfield in a railroad station on July 2, 1881, and Garfield died from those wounds on Sept. 19, 1881—just six months after taking office. The nation mourned a president it was just getting to know, and contributions poured in to his widow, Lucretia, who used the money to add a memorial wing to **Lawnfield**, the Garfield home in Mentor. The press had dubbed the home Lawnfield during the 1880 campaign, though neither Garfield nor his wife was particularly fond of the name.

Garfield had purchased the property in 1876, describing it at that time as a "dilapidated farmhouse on 119 acres." The Garfields spent four years renovating and expanding the home, with work continuing even during the presidential campaign. After the president's death, Lucretia had plans for a memorial wing drawn, making one stipulation—the new additions could not alter the older section of the home that her husband had built and loved. After Mrs. Garfield's death, Lawnfield continued to be occupied until the late 1920s by her brother, Joseph Rudolph. In 1938, the house was opened as a historic site.

The first two floors of the estate still contain the Garfields' furnishings and possessions. Family portraits decorate the walls, and period pieces typical of those of an upper-middle-class family in the late 1800s are throughout the house. Perhaps the most impressive room is the formal library Lucretia added to Lawnfield, which features blond white oak beams, fireplace mantle, and ceiling and has two large alcoves.

The third floor houses a museum, complete with political cartoons, banners, and posters from 1880—even a set of Garfield campaign cufflinks! Other items include Horatio Alger's book about Garfield, *From Canal Boy to President*, which stressed Garfield's humble beginnings (though he worked on the canal for only two months). Also displayed are Garfield's Civil War gun, sword, boots, and uniform.

Lawnfield is on Rte. 20 (Mentor Avenue) between Rtes. 306 and 615, Mentor; (216) 255-8722. Open Tuesday through Saturday, 10 A.M.–5 P.M.; Sunday and holidays, noon–5 P.M. Admission: adults, $3; children (ages six–twelve) and senior citizens, $1.50.

The Debevcs have made wine for family and friends for three generations, but it wasn't until 1970 that Tony Sr. and Tony Jr. decided to convert some of their farm acreage into a commercial vineyard. **Chalet Debonne Vineyards** produced its first bottle for sale in 1972, and near constant expansion has taken place ever since. With nearly a half million dollars invested in the latest winery equipment, the Debevcs hired Tony Carlucci, believed to be the first California winemaker to take up residence at an Ohio winery.

Guests at Chalet Debonne sample the nine varieties of Debevc wine—four white wines, two roses, and three red wines—in a Swiss-style A-frame chalet with a large fireplace, red checkered tablecloths, and weathered barn board siding on the inside walls. Visitors may also sit under the grapevines on the patio during warm weather, and snacks such as cheese and sausage plates and homemade bread are served. Polka bands perform on Wednesday and Friday evenings.

Tours of the winery take place hourly, or as needed, with members of the Debevc family explaining the various steps in wine making, from grape crushing and filtering, to aging and bottling. The large cellar holds 60,000 gallons of wine in various stages of fermentation.

Chalet Debonne Vineyards is 3 miles west of Rte. 534 on South River Road, Madison; (216) 466-3485. Open Tuesday, Thursday, and Saturday, 1–8 P.M.; Wednesday and Friday, 1 P.M.–midnight. Closed in January. No blue jeans permitted after 8 P.M.

Acres of vineyards can be seen throughout eastern Lake County, and five minutes from Chalet Debonne is another winery: **Grand River Vineyard**. After driving past the rows of grapevines, you reach a modern building at the edge of a cool forest. Unlike other wineries, Grand River continuously changes the wines it produces, so customers have the opportunity to taste new variations and blends on each visit to this pleasant facility.

Grand River Vineyard is at 5750 Madison Road (Rte. 528), Madison; (216) 298-9838. Open Monday, Tuesday, and Thursday, 1–8 P.M.; Wednesday, 1–11 P.M.; Friday and Saturday, 1–6 P.M.

A restaurant at the Lake-Ashtabula county line rests on the site of one of the early log buildings in the Western Reserve. Originally known as the Webster House, the cabin was built in 1798 and measured only 12 by 15 feet, yet it was a popular stop for settlers heading west in covered wagons on the trail from Pittsburgh.

In later years, the name was changed to the New England House, and finally to its present name, the **Old Tavern**. Innkeepers expanded the tavern several times during the 1800s, and the four massive pillars were added to the front of the building in 1820.

Decorated in an Early American motif, the Old Tavern continues the tradition of serving generous portions of hearty country cooking. Dinner entrees include roast round of choice beef, country fried chicken, and baked stuffed pork chop. From the sea, the Old Tavern offers fantail shrimp, deep sea scallops, roast duck, and African lobster tail. Dinner entrees are served with a salad, biscuits and jelly, choice of potato, and delicious corn fritters—warm corn bread and kernels formed into a ball and topped with maple syrup and powdered sugar. The fresh desserts are all prepared on the premises. The rhubarb pie is a house specialty, and the grasshopper pie (creme de menthe cream pie) is exceptional. Enjoy an after-dinner cocktail in the new Coach House Pub.

The Old Tavern is just inside the Lake County line on Rte. 84, Unionville; (216) 428-2091. Open Monday through Saturday, 11 A.M.–9 P.M.; Sunday, noon–7 P.M. Prices: lunch, inexpensive to moderate; dinner, moderate to expensive. MasterCard and Visa are accepted.

Ashtabula County

Restoration is underway in the **Ashtabula Harbor area**, and twenty-six buildings have already been listed on the National Register of Historic Places. Ashtabula's heyday as a port has long since passed, but a new breed of merchants has created a charming shopping district in the 100-year-old structures on Bridge Street, just up the hill from an unusual lift bridge. During Ashtabula's years as a thriving shipping center, it was said to have more saloons than any other port in the world except one—Singapore.

Amid the antique and gift shops is a pleasant and reasonably priced place to dine—**Hulbert's Restaurant**. Ceiling fans slowly spin near the high, molded plaster ceiling, and exposed brick interior walls create a turn-of-the-century atmosphere. The dining tables and chairs are an eclectic mix of antiques and contemporary pieces, and the effect is very pleasing. Fresh flowers dress up each table, and a large brick archway connects the two dining areas, which were once separate buildings. Owners Fred and Elaine Swanson use wall space at Hulbert's to display the work of Ohio artists; many feature harbor scenes and other local points of interest; some are available for purchase. A recent addition here is the Victorian garden in the rear courtyard.

Hulbert's lunch menu offers a wide variety of sandwiches, including the hot, open-faced Drake sandwich (made famous at Chicago's Drake Hotel), which consists of ham, turkey, and sliced tomatoes, topped with melted Swiss and cheddar cheeses. Other luncheon selections range from soups and salads to quiche and the unique cheese-stuffed flounder.

At the dinner hour, choose from two dozen entree selections— steaks, seafood, Southern fried chicken, liver and grilled onions, and more. For a tasty appetizer, try the crisp chicken wings, served hot, medium, or mild with two zesty sauces.

19

Hulbert's Restaurant

Baking is a special tradition at Hulbert's—twenty kinds of homemade pies tempt diners every day here. From-scratch muffins are served with every meal, and fresh cinnamon rolls and eggs benedict are featured for Sunday breakfast. Choco-holics of the world, try the chocolate suicide cake—deep chocolate cake surrounded with chocolate butter cream, then topped with chocolate glaze and chocolate bits. This one is a real diet buster!

Hulbert's Restaurant is at 1033 Bridge Street, Ashtabula; (216) 964-2594. Open Tuesday through Thursday, 11 A.M.–8 P.M.; Friday and Saturday, 11 A.M.–9 P.M.; Sunday, 8 A.M.–8 P.M. Prices: lunch, inexpensive; dinner, moderate to expensive. Personal checks are accepted.

After your meal, drop by the **Navajo Corner**, a Bridge Street shop loaded with turquoise and silver jewelry, pottery, and Indian blankets. **Four Flags of Scandia** features unique gifts from Denmark, Finland, Norway, and Sweden.

One of my favorite Bridge Street stops is Paul Daley's **Circa 1889** antique shop. Daley opened Circa 1889 (which is named for the year this former dry goods store was built) in 1981. He specializes in area antiques and nautical items. When I last visited, Daley had a magnificent carved oak back bar, 18 feet long by nearly 10 feet high, which had come from an East 15th Street tavern. This massive piece included a matching front bar and icebox and was priced at $15,000.

In addition to the unique inventory, Daley, a fifth-generation Ashtabula resident, has a local yarn about many of the shop's items. He is a direct descendant of William Brewster, elder of Plymouth and signer of the Mayflower Compact in 1620. A large etching of the signing of the Mayflower Compact hangs in Paul's shop. Daley also claims Clarence Darrow as a distant relative, and he has a book written by the famous attorney and author that was printed by the Roycrafters in 1897. Darrow practiced law in the Ashtabula area.

Circa 1889 is at 1005 Bridge Street, Ashtabula. Open daily from 11 A.M. to 6 P.M., but Paul often can be found in the shop at other hours as well.

Off the Beaten Path
in East Central Ohio

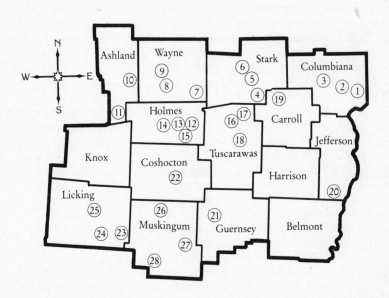

1. Beaver Creek State Park
2. Lock 24 Restaurant
3. Fort Tuscarora Museum
4. Cibo's Restaurant
5. Canton Classic Car Museum
6. Hoover Historical Center
7. Lehman Hardware
8. Pine Tree Barn
9. Quailcrest Farm, Herb Barn, and Country Gallery
10. Delagrange Antiques
11. Mohican State Park/Blackfork Inn
12. Amish Home
13. Helping Hands Quilt Shop
14. Rastetter Woolen Mill/Inn at Honey Run
15. Troyer's Homestead Restaurant/Guggisberg Cheese
16. Warther's
17. Zoar Village
18. Schoenbrunn Village
19. Conestoga Farm
20. Friends Meeting House
21. Degenhart Paperweight and Glass Museum/Mosser Glass
22. Roscoe Village
23. Flint Ridge
24. Dawes Arboretum
25. Granville/Ye Olde Mill
26. Longaberger Basket Company
27. National Road-Zane Grey Museum
28. Robinson-Ransbottom Pottery Company

East Central Ohio

Columbiana County

Stunning natural beauty and re-created pioneer history blend together in a state park in the foothills of the Appalachians— **Beaver Creek State Park**. Wide, swift Little Beaver Creek rushes through deep gorges, past pine and fir forests, the locks of the old Sandy and Beaver Canal, and a restored pioneer village.

Private entrepreneurs constructed the canal between 1834 and 1848, connecting the Ohio River with the Ohio and Erie Canal. Though they spent $3 million on the project by its completion, the canal carried paying traffic only until 1852, when competition from the railroad doomed the canal era in this part of the state. Ironically, the directors of the Sandy and Beaver kept the Pennsylvania Railroad out of the county to avoid competition between the railroad and their canal—a move that had dire consequences for the canal towns in Columbiana County after the Sandy and Beaver failed.

Fifteen miles of hiking trails and numerous bridle trails follow Little Beaver Creek and wind through the woods up the steep foothills. Canoe rentals nearby provide the equipment for those who wish to take on the challenging creek, and primitive camping areas are scattered throughout the 3,000-acre park. The creek offers anglers a variety of fish, including smallmouth and rock bass.

Gaston's Mill, built by Samuel Conkle in 1830, dominates the park's reconstructed pioneer village. Originally powered by a large waterwheel, the mill operated until 1920, though in later years it used steam and gas engines to drive the massive grinding stones. When restored, it was converted back to waterwheel power, and on summer weekends visitors observe the mill at work and may purchase stone-ground corn, wheat, and buckwheat flour. A pioneer church, schoolhouse, cabin, and blacksmith shop, all filled with antiques from Ohio's early settlement era, surround the historic mill.

Beaver Creek State Park is off Rte. 7, 15 miles east of Lisbon; (216) 385-3091. Open year-round.

Rural Columbiana County seems an unlikely spot for a quality continental restaurant, but **Lock 24** is precisely that. The Pugh family restored a barn built in the 1830s, and the rustic beams of the original structure are plainly visible in the entry, lounge, and main dining area. Before-and-after photos document the comprehensive restoration of this attractive restaurant, which takes its name from the canal lock behind the building near the middle fork of Little Beaver Creek. A cheerful glassed-in sun porch, decorated with ceiling fans, Tiffany lamps, and both boxed and hanging plants, provides the perfect setting for lunch in the country.

Lock 24's luncheon menu features soups and salads, including salad nicoise, which is a mix of light tuna and fresh steamed vegetables tossed in vinaigrette dressing and garnished with ripe olives and hard-boiled egg. Or feast on the Ultimate Salad—white asparagus spears, hearts of palm, watercress, cucumbers, and ripe olives, served with Lock 24's special dressing. Other lunch offerings include omelets, hot and cold sandwiches, seafood and pasta, beef and potato cake, broiled catch of the day, and the intriguing chicken renaissance—chicken, egg noodle, mushroom, chives in a sherry sauce, all breaded and baked.

Unlike many country dining establishments with standard American fare, Lock 24 prides itself on serving sophisticated dinner entrees such as steak au poivre (a strip steak coated with black pepper and a brandied cream sauce), shrimp dijon, chicken grand marnier, and boeuf au fromage (sliced tenderloin lightly breaded, pan fried in butter, then broiled with Roquefort and Parmesan cheeses). The menu features a variety of other innovative dishes, including the delightful sea scallops and gulf shrimp, which are marinated in olive oil, dry vermouth, and shallots, and then broiled and served in a distinctive tomato–white butter sauce.

A Lock 24 dinner salad comes loaded with radishes, carrots, cucumbers, and tomato, and the homemade breads, particularly the carrot and pumpkin muffins, are outstanding. Banana bread pudding, New York–style cheesecake, poached pear with custard rum sauce and double fudge chocolate sauce, and creme au caramel are but a sampling of the exotic dessert creations served here.

In addition to the excellent kitchen, Lock 24 offers travelers two shops for browsing. The Lock Loft Gallery features the work of eighty-five artists—everything from paintings to a wide selection of crafts. Raspberry Soup is a complete gift shop.

Lock 24 is on Rte. 154, 1 mile east of Rte. 11, near Elkton; (216) 424-3710. Open Tuesday through Friday, 11:30 A.M.–10 P.M.; Saturday, 11:30 A.M.–3 P.M., 5–10 P.M. Prices: lunch, inexpensive to moderate; dinner, moderate to expensive. Visa, MasterCard, and American Express are accepted. Reservations are recommended.

T. W. Pike collected antique guns and Indian artifacts for years, mounting old muskets, swords, and arrowhead collections on the walls of his home. By the early 1950s he had run out of wall (and closet) space, so he embarked on an ambitious project—building his own museum. His replica of an early American blockhouse, constructed of rough timber and stone, opened as the **Fort Tuscarora Museum** in 1959. Fort Tuscarora also contains Tom Pike's gun shop, and he has a target range out the back door.

In addition to the impressive collection of rifles and pistols, the museum displays British military swords and coins from the French and Indian War, bullets from the Civil War battle at Gettysburg, and cannon balls used at Fredericksburg. Fort Tuscarora has Civil War uniforms and belt buckles from both the Union and Confederate armies and Indian artifacts, including extensive collections of weapon points, craftwork, and paintings.

The second floor of the museum houses furniture and farm implements used by early settlers in the area, plus blacksmith tools and household items such as butter churns and an 1820 sausage grinder. Many of the items on display, including the pioneer bedroom exhibit, are from the area around Guilford Lake, which was built as a reservoir for the Sandy and Beaver Canal in 1832.

Tom Pike's gun shop sells kits, powder, caps, and accessories for muzzle-loading rifles and sidearms, new and used modern firearms, and a complete selection of leather goods such as belts, holsters, and Indian dolls.

The Fort Tuscarora Museum is on Rte. 172, 6 miles west of Lisbon; (216) 222-1666. The museum is open Monday through Friday, 4–8 P.M.; Saturday, 10 A.M.–5 P.M.; and Sunday 1–5 P.M. Admission: adults, $1; children (under age twelve), 25¢.

Stark County

Rena Rugani's **Cibo's Restaurant** serves authentic Italian cooking in a very unusual setting—an old movie theater. The

Mohawk Theater, built in the early 1940s, presented feature films for the people of Waynesburg for decades. But since 1971, it has been spaghetti, not spaghetti Westerns, that attracts crowds at 134 West Lisbon Street.

At first, dining was limited to the Mohawk's old lobby, but now the entire theater has been remodeled and converted to a multi-level eating area, complete with ceiling fans and oak dividers. Italian favorites such as antipasto, pasta fagioli (bean) and spezzato (wedding) soup, and homemade chicken noodles constitute the list of appetizers. The reasonably priced entrees include spaghetti, rigatoni, cavatelli, lasagna, ravioli, and cannelloni or, for those who have trouble choosing from that list, a combination plate offers a sample of all of the above. Cibo's offers American dishes as well—steaks and chicken, plus family-style combinations of spaghetti, ravioli, chicken, lasagna, and steak. Pizza and sandwiches are also served.

Cibo's is at 134 West Lisbon Street, Waynesburg; (216) 866-3838. Open Thursday through Sunday, 11 A.M.–8 P.M. Prices: inexpensive to moderate. Personal checks are accepted.

For those who appreciate the rumble seats, wooden-spoke wheels, and V-16 engines of antique automobiles, a stop at the **Canton Classic Car Museum** is a must. The museum comprises dozens of meticulously restored vehicles, from a bright red 1921 Pierce Arrow tow truck to a 1938 Cadillac convertible with a 452-cubic-inch, 185-horsepower engine.

Six Packard automobiles, from model years between 1920 and 1949, trace the evolution of that distinctive make. For elegant driving, the museum contains a pair of Rolls Royces—a red and white 1929 Phantom I convertible and a 1938 Phantom III with open driver's compartment. The museum also has a rare Marmon Sixteen which, according to an advertisement used at a 1931 automobile show, "looks and performs like no other car—16 cylinders, 200 horsepower and under $5000."

The two-seat 1929 Kissel White Eagle Speedster (available with rumble seat) conjures up images of goggles, blowing scarves, and deserted country roads. The very rare 1914 Benham is the only survivor of the nineteen cars produced by this short-lived automaker, which folded after only one year in business.

In addition to the fine old cars, vintage gas and steam engines and other automotive paraphernalia are on display. In the restoration shop, future classics await rejuvenation.

27

Canton Classic Car Museum

The Canton Classic Car Museum is at 555 Market Avenue South, Canton; (216) 455-3603. Open May through October, Tuesday through Sunday, 10 A.M.–5 P.M.; November through April, Friday through Sunday, 10 A.M.–5 P.M. Admission: adults, $3; children, $1.

Daniel and Mary Hoover arrived on their eighty-two–acre farm in 1840, and on this farm Daniel founded the family's leather tannery. The enterprise prospered and eventually was moved into the town of North Canton. Daniel's son, W. H. Hoover, realized at the turn of the century that the coming age of automobiles would drastically reduce the demand for leather goods such as harnesses and saddles. So W. H. Hoover searched for a new product for the Hoover Company and discovered it when he bought the rights to inventor Murray Spangler's upright vacuum cleaner. In 1908, Hoover offered the public the first commercially viable upright vacuum cleaner, the Hoover Suction Sweeper Model O.

From that successful product, the Hoover Company blossomed into an international concern in less than a decade. With its world headquarters in North Canton, the company has established the **Hoover Historical Center** on the family's original Stark County farmstead.

An eight-minute audiovisual presentation details the history of the company, and guided tours begin in the original tannery, where many leather-working tools and artifacts from the late 1800s are displayed. The two-story white farmhouse contains what has to be the world's most complete collection of antique vacuums, ranging from the 1869 Whirlwind Cleaner, the first vacuum cleaner offered for sale, to modern Hoover units.

The Kotten Suction Cleaner, built in 1910, required the operator to stand and rock on the bellows to create suction—it sold for $25. The 1905 Skinner electric vacuum was advertised as a portable, but weighed over a hundred pounds! Murray Spangler's original 1907 upright stands next to the Hoover Model O, which launched this multinational corporation. Other Hoover exhibits include old photos of W. H. Hoover and various Hoover factories around the world, early newspaper and magazine advertisements for Hoover products, and some furnishings used by the family in the farmhouse. Herb and flower gardens surround the museum.

The Hoover Historical Center is at 2225 Easton Street, North Canton; (216) 499-0287. Open Tuesday through Sunday, 1–5 P.M. No admission charge.

Wayne County

Ohio's largest Amish and Swiss Mennonite communities are in four east central Ohio counties: Holmes, Wayne, Tuscarawas, and Stark. The Amish espouse a simple agrarian lifestyle and reject the use of automobiles and electricity as potentially disruptive to that lifestyle. Living in the twentieth century without electricity creates a demand for unusual products, such as kerosene-powered refrigerators, and one Wayne County business, **Lehman Hardware**, has established itself as the non-electric appliance and equipment supplier for the area's substantial Amish population.

While Lehman's stocks the nails, wire, and garden tools found in every hardware store, the bulk of the floorspace is dedicated to merchandise such as gas-powered washing machines and gas and kerosene lamps. Wood- and coal-burning cooking and heating stoves fill one large showroom, with many of the cooking stoves ornately trimmed in chrome and costing up to $2,500. Used cooking stoves (trade-ins) are also available.

Other items in Lehman's inventory include hardwood fruit presses, an apple parer, a cherry stoner, and a bottle capper. How many other stores carry a variety of hand-crank butter churns and a hand-powered cream separator that produces eighty-five liters of milk per hour?

The store's crowded hitching posts, used by the Amish to secure their horse-drawn buggies, indicate the popularity of Lehman Hardware with the local Amish population, but in recent years Lehman's has attracted another type of customer—people drawn to wood- and coal-burning appliances because of the increasing cost of utilities. Lehman's sells an eighty-page catalog called *Lehman's Non-Electric Good Neighbor Heritage Catalog* for $2. It's full of major appliances, small gristmills, copper wash boilers, sausage stuffers, noodle makers, and carbide lamps. And city people have been known to purchase unique non-electric devices, particularly the fancy chrome cooking stoves, simply for use as decorative pieces.

Lehman Hardware is 2 miles west of Rte. 94 in downtown Kidron; (216) 857-5441. Open Monday through Saturday, 7 A.M.– 5:30 P.M.; Thursday until 9 P.M.

After establishing their Christmas tree farm, Robert and Roger Dush's next challenge was to convert a barn built in the 1860s into a Christmas shop and country store, the **Pine Tree Barn**. This massive old barn has been designated a Wayne County Historic Landmark, and its original rough-hewn beams and floors create a rustic atmosphere.

Divided into several distinct areas, the barn's Christmas shop stocks quality ornaments and decorative pieces imported from Austria, Germany, England, and Scandinavia, including unusual handcrafted wooden pieces such as the popular pyramids and smoking men. The smoking men are incense burners carved in the shapes of appealing German folk characters who puff their pipes and expel the smoke through their tiny mouths. The rising heat of burning candles turns the pyramids' wooden propellers, thus providing power for these miniature carousels.

In the loft, you'll discover the Farm Kitchen, filled with hand-crafted baskets, salt-glazed pottery, and many other kitchen items. In the Children's Barn, you'll delight at the offerings—old-fashioned toys, dolls, and stuffed animals that bring back wonderful memories.

The lower level of the barn, once a stable, now holds the Flower Shop. Dried flowers, baskets, pottery, and supplies are in abundance. A few steps take you into the greenhouse, alive with blooms and greenery.

The old grain bin has been transformed into a small kitchen, serving a light lunch of quiche, sandwiches, homemade breads, and fresh desserts Tuesday through Saturday from 11:30 A.M. to 2 P.M. Large windows along the back wall of the barn provide those eating lunch with a view down the hill to the private forty-acre lake and rows of young Christmas trees. Diners also see antique farm implements mounted on the walls of the barn and the block and tackle that once hauled bales of hay up from the ground level to the second-floor loft.

The Pine Tree Barn is on Rte. 226, 4 miles south of Wooster, (216) 264-1014. Open Tuesday through Sunday, 10 A.M.–5 P.M. Closed in January.

Set in rolling Wayne County farmland is charming **Quailcrest Farm**. More than four hundred different herbs and perennial plants, both potted and field grown, are cultivated here, ready for transplanting to your backyard garden. Shrubs and trees are also available. March through June is the peak season for plants at Quailcrest, but a good selection is available throughout the summer and into fall.

In addition to two working greenhouses, Quailcrest has three shops for visitors to explore. Inside the Country Gallery (right behind the Bruch family farmhouse), an extensive selection of hand-thrown pottery competes for attention with copper pieces, weavings, carved and painted decoys, baskets, puzzles, and games. Children's gifts and books fill a second-floor loft.

Down the walk through a flower-lined pergola you will find the new Herb Barn, which replaces the barn and shop destroyed by fire in 1986. Herb products, garden books and cookbooks, pewter, herb wreaths, woven rugs, and decorative pieces all are available here. The Plant Barn, large and airy, features sculptures and benches for your garden, terra cotta, and farm-grown dried flowers.

Browsers will enjoy five acres of display gardens overlooking the Killbuck Valley. Included are three herb gardens, a circular perennial garden, and an English garden. The first Saturday after Labor Day marks a popular annual event—the Quailcrest Farm

Herb Fair. More than forty crafts people exhibit the fruits of their labors, including pottery, baskets, and culinary herbs and arrangements. Lunch is served, and visitors observe craft demonstrations such as basket weaving and natural dyeing.

Quailcrest Farm is off Rte. 83 at 2810 Armstrong Road, 6 miles north of Wooster (7 miles south of I-71); (216) 345-6722. Open mid-March through December, Tuesday through Saturday, 10 A.M.–5 P.M. (open Sundays, 1–5 P.M., in May and December).

Ashland County

Out-of-state antique dealers have frequented Jeromesville, Ohio, for years, but most native Ohioans are unaware of the town's reputation as an antique stop. George Delagrange owns one of Jeromesville's more intriguing shops, **Delagrange Antiques**, which is in an 1870s storefront that originally housed the town's drugstore.

Delagrange's fifteen-year-old business specializes in the poplar, cherry, and walnut pieces so in demand with East Coast buyers. Delagrange (whose name means "from the farm" in French) purchases four-poster rope spring beds, cupboards, tables, and chests from area farms, selling hundreds of major pieces each year. In addition, Delagrange has an extensive inventory of exquisite handmade quilts. George and his wife, Susan, always are delighted to chat with visitors about tidbits of local history that pertain to the pieces in their shop.

Delagrange Antiques is at 12 North High Street, Jeromesville; (419) 368-8371. Open daily except Wednesdays, 9 A.M.–5 P.M.; Sundays, noon–5 P.M.

The natural beauty of the Mohican area, with its steep and rolling hills, swift rivers, and deep forests, once prompted world-famous author Louis Bromfield to remark, "I live on the edge of paradise." Visitors to the area quickly realize that statement was no exaggeration. White pines flourish along the ridges of the Mohican State Park and State Forest, while hemlock abounds in the hollows and gorges.

Cabins in Ohio's state parks are typically located in scenic surroundings, but the twenty-five two-bedroom **Mohican State Park cabins**, isolated from the rest of the park in woodlands along the bank of Clear Fork Creek, may just be in the most picturesque setting of any cabins in Ohio. They come furnished with all linens, blankets, and kitchen equipment and may be rented in the summer for full weeks only. (There are no restrictions on the length of stay the rest of the year.) Canoeing and rafting are favorite summertime activities on Clear Fork Creek, and hiking, fishing, and camping are also popular in the park.

Mohican State Park Cabins are on Rte. 3, just north of Rte. 97, Loudonville; (419) 994-4290. Open year-round. Rates range from $48 for the first day to $198 per week. Early reservations are a must.

Another lodging option in the lush Mohican State Park and State Forest is the impressive stone and timber **Mohican Lodge** perched on a bluff overlooking Pleasant Hill Lake. Each room in the lodge has a private balcony or patio, many with views of either the woods surrounding the lodge or the lake. Facilities include an indoor and outdoor pool, two tennis courts, shuffleboard, and a game room. In addition to the meals served in the dining room, pool-side barbecues are offered occasionally during summer months.

The Mohican State Park Lodge is on Rte. 97, 6 miles west of Loudonville; (419) 938-5411. Open year-round. Rates: $71 per night, double occupancy.

The confluence of Black Fork River and Clear Fork Creek forms the scenic Mohican River, probably Ohio's most popular stream for canoeing, kayaking, and rafting. Canoe liveries rent hundreds of canoes and kayaks in the Loudonville area, from as early as April to as late as November. With prices of $9 per canoe and up, and trips lasting from two hours to several days, these liveries provide access to these scenic waterways. Two such liveries are within walking distance of one another on Rte. 3, south of Loudonville and north of Rte. 97: **Mohican River Canoe Livery**, (419) 994-4020, and **Mohican Canoe Livery**, (419) 994-4097. Many others operate in the area, and a complete list is available from the Loudonville Chamber of Commerce, Loudonville, Ohio 44842; (419) 994-5225.

Another enjoyable way to explore the 4,000-acre Mohican State Forest is on horseback, and **Bit 'N Bridle Stables** offers guided trail rides through sections of this vast wooded preserve. Along the paths, riders enjoy the deer, rabbits, and multicolored wildflowers in this peaceful state forest. Trail rides cost $11.50 for the first hour. For groups of ten or more, Bit 'N Bridle gives hayrides for $4 per person.

Bit 'N Bridle Stables is at 996 County Road #3275, off Rte. 3

south of Rte. 97, Perrysville; (419) 938-8681. Open May through September, Tuesday through Sunday, 9 A.M.–dark (open daily from Memorial Day to Labor Day).

It's a dream you may have had, too: Purchase one of those charming Victorian houses on a quiet street in a small Ohio town and restore it to create the perfect bed and breakfast. City people would flock to your new establishment, attracted by the charm of your stately residence, not to mention your gracious hospitality. You would earn extra income while enjoying the company of "new friends."

I'm sure that's what the couple who originally restored the **Blackfork Inn** believed when they purchased this 1865-vintage property on Water Street in Loudonville. Built by Philip J. Black, this delightful brick, three-story home seemed destined to be a fine small inn. And the couple restoring it decided to "do it right" by importing antiques from Europe, installing a complete commercial kitchen, securing accurate reproductions of period wallpapers, and updating the six guest rooms with private baths, while retaining the high ceilings and natural woodwork that make such properties both distinctive and desirable. It's rumored they spent upwards of a half-million dollars on this project, and that may have been their undoing. Less than a year from their grand opening, the Blackfork Inn was closed down and boarded up—its brief resurrection snuffed out.

On Labor Day weekend in 1982, Al and Sue Gorisek arrived at the sheriff's auction at the Blackfork hoping to pick up some good deals on antiques, which they have collected for years. But they walked away as the proud new owners of the entire inn.

Philip Black built his home from the profits he made during the Civil War selling groceries and such to Federal troops. It's said he was instrumental in bringing the railroad to Loudonville, so it seems appropriate that railroad tracks are next door—it's the main line between New York and Chicago, so trains do rumble by!

Both Goriseks are in publishing: Al is an editor for the *Cleveland Plain Dealer*, Sue writes for *Ohio Magazine*. And the Blackfork has become Sue's other career—she splits her time between their home in Cleveland and the inn. Sue is perhaps the perfect host for such a place, for as an *Ohio Magazine* senior correspondent, she travels the state extensively and has plenty of tips for guests on where to go and what to see in the area.

Blackfork Inn

Accommodations at the Blackfork Inn include a fine continental breakfast. Although no other meals are routinely served, an area chef is available to prepare elegant meals for guests, with approximately one week's notice.

The Blackfork Inn is at 303 North Water Street, Loudonville; (419) 994-3252. Rates: $43 single, $62 double. MasterCard and Visa are accepted. Open year-round.

Holmes County

The fertile, rolling farmland of Holmes County is the center of Ohio's largest Amish community, with 20,000 of the 70,000 Amish in the United States living in the area. Amish men and women, dressed in plain, solid-colored clothing, can be seen in the markets, restaurants, and shops, or driving their black, horse-drawn buggies through the pastoral countryside.

Amish restaurants in Holmes and surrounding counties serve simple country cooking at reasonable prices, and shops sell Amish goods, such as quilts. This section of east central Ohio also contains a sizable Swiss Mennonite population, and there are many cheese houses producing Swiss cheese from the milk brought in by Amish dairy farmers.

The Amish split with the Mennonite Church in 1609 to follow the leadership of Jacob Amman, from whom the sect gets its name. Facing religious persecution in their native Germany and Switzerland, they began a migration to the United States in the mid-1700s, settling first in Pennsylvania, where many Amish live today. The move to Ohio took place in the 1820s, and the Amish have continued their agricultural traditions for the past 150 years.

Gloria and Eli Yoder's **Amish Home** is a 100-acre working farm that can be explored by visitors to Amish country. Children will enjoy the horses, rabbits, chickens, sheep, cows, pigs, and goats that fill the barn. Adults will probably be more interested in the two farmhouses, both built more than a hundred years ago. The first home on your tour contains furnishings typical of an Amish farmhouse in the late 1800s. Built in 1866, this home last served as a residence thirty years ago. Its wood floors, simple heavy furniture, wood-burning cook stove, and people-powered appliances (such as a pump sewing machine) give a glimpse of the lifestyle of Amish farm families.

The larger home at the Amish Home, constructed in 1885 and occupied for 100 years, is similarly furnished but contains some unusual items such as gas floor lamps. Religious services have been held here many times, as in most Amish homes and barns. These services take three full hours to complete.

Many who visit here enjoy buggy tours of the property, which even has a hilltop family cemetery. Inside the craft shop, you'll discover quilts, dolls, pottery, woodwork, and many other country favorites. And be sure to pick up a copy of the *Downhome Shoppers Guide*. This 100-page magazinelike publication is *the* guide to Ohio's Amish settlements. It's packed with information on Amish restaurants, tours, crafts, quilts, cheese, and the like, with hundreds of entries and very detailed maps.

Yoder's Amish Home is on Rte. 515 between Trail and Walnut Creek; (216) 893-2541. Open April through October, Monday through Saturday, 10 A.M.–5:30 P.M. Tours: adults, $2.50; children, $1.25. Buggy rides: adults, $2; children, $1.

If you admire fine, handmade quilts, stop by the **Helping Hands Quilt Shop**. A non-profit enterprise with all proceeds donated to charities and missions, the shop stocks hundreds of marvelous quilts in every conceivable pattern and color combination. Many of these are sewn in the large, sunlit quilting room in the back of the shop, where Helping Hands serves a social function in addition to its contributions to charity.

Helping Hands will quilt your quilt top, custom design a quilt for you, or even finish a quilt you have already started. The shop also sells quilted pillow covers, quilting books, embroidery kits and floss, quilting needles, thread, fabrics, stencils, and patterns—in short, everything a quilter could need.

The Helping Hands Quilt Shop is on Rte. 39 in Berlin; (216) 893-2410. Open Monday through Saturday, 9 A.M.–5 P.M.

The **Rastetter Woolen Mill** has been in the family for more than one hundred years, and Tim and Maureen Rastetter now operate the business. The mill custom makes fine wool and down comforters, which they sell through their mill store or by mail. Rastetter also custom weaves rugs and carpet in just about any size, shape, or pattern, with a catalog of their best-selling patterns available.

The mill provides wool washing and carding and purchases wool from individuals all over the country. Other items in the mill store include wool and down jackets, wool blankets and socks, coverlets, and spinning wheel kits.

The Rastetter Woolen Mill is on Rtes. 39 and 62 between Millersburg and Berlin; (216) 674-2103. Open Tuesday through Saturday, noon–5 P.M. (closed all of January and on Tuesdays, February through May).

When I first heard about a "modern" inn that opened outside Millersburg, right in the heart of Amish country, I must admit I was skeptical. I envisioned a motel-like structure on a bulldozed and paved chunk of earth, and I wasn't thrilled by the prospect.

The Inn at Honey Run does not fit that description in the least. As you motor up a winding county road, through dense vegetation, your curiosity can't help but be aroused. And when you reach the tasteful contemporary structure that is the Inn at Honey Run, it's difficult not to let out a sigh of approval. Carefully blended into the surrounding trees—trees so close that I'm not sure how they managed to get the inn up without disturbing them—is a truly unique getaway. Lots of exposed wood, inside and out, creates a harmony between the inn and the peaceful forest. The inn's twenty-five guest rooms combine a potpourri of styles—everything from Shaker and Early American to very contemporary. Cherry, pine, oak, and walnut furnishings complete these rooms; some feature bi-level floor plans with skylights. All have living areas and tabletop space for work (if absolutely necessary), writing, card playing, or whatever.

If you can't stay the night, then come by and enjoy an excellent meal in the dining room, which has a wall of glass for viewing the trees and wild flowers. Amish quilts hang on the walls, and many of the servers are Amish as well. The inn prides itself on its from-scratch recipes, including some spectacular pastries and desserts, and regional specialties like Holmes County pan-fried trout. The dining room is open to all for lunch and dinner, by reservation, Monday through Saturday. Overnight guests have the place to themselves on Sundays.

The Inn at Honey Run is 3 miles northeast of Millersburg, off Rte. 241 on County Road 203; (800) 468-6639 (in Ohio), (216) 674-0011. Lodging rates: $50 to $150 per night for two people, including breakfast. Visa, MasterCard, and American Express are accepted. Open year-round.

Charm is the state's only predominately Amish town, and evidence of that fact includes the popularity of the local icehouse (since the Amish don't use electric refrigerators), the town's harness shop (for the horse-drawn buggies and field horses' leather needs), and the hitching posts behind the popular **Troyer's Homestead Restaurant**.

Troyer's is not the largest Amish restaurant in the county, nor the fanciest, but it does serve authentic Amish cooking at reasonable prices. The menu features a variety of sandwiches, and the dinner entrees include country favorites such as fried chicken, pork chops, steaks, ham, and fish. Family-style dinners of chicken, roast beef, and ham, or any combination of the three, include a choice of vegetables and potatoes. Fresh desserts are one of the trademarks of Amish restaurants, and Troyer's is no exception, offering very tasty peanut butter cream and pecan pies, plus date pudding, sundaes, and Amish cracker pudding. Homemade breads and pastries are also available to carry out.

Troyer's Homestead Restaurant is on Rte. 557 in Charm; (216) 893-2717. Open Monday through Saturday, 7 A.M.–8 P.M. Prices: inexpensive to moderate.

Just up the road from Troyer's is the "Home of Ohio Baby Swiss Cheese," the **Guggisberg Cheese Company**, owned and operated by Alfred and Margaret Guggisberg. Born in Switzerland, Alfred began work in a cheese factory more than forty years ago at the age of sixteen.

Today, their plant produces 1,000 five-pound wheels of baby Swiss each day between 10 A.M. and noon, cheese which is then shipped worldwide. Local Amish dairy farmers supply the milk to Guggisberg, which arrives daily in horse-pulled buggies. Visitors to the plant can see the cheese forming in large stainless-steel vats by looking through the windows that connect the plant with the retail store. Guggisberg stocks a wide variety of cheeses in addition to Ohio baby Swiss, and cuckoo clocks, books, gift items, and ice cream are also sold.

Guggisberg Cheese is on Rte. 557, north of Charm; (216) 893-2500. Open during warm months Monday through Friday, 8 A.M.–6 P.M.; Saturday, 8 A.M.–8 P.M.; Sunday, 11 A.M.–4 P.M. Open the rest of the year Monday through Saturday, 8 A.M.–5 P.M.

Tuscarawas County

Europe's foremost woodcarvers proclaimed Ernest Warther "the world's master carver," and the intricately crafted carvings displayed at **Warther's** museum give credence to that proclamation. Born near Dover, Ohio, in 1885, Ernest started carving at age five, when he found an old pocket knife while tending the family's cow. His formal education ended in the second grade, and at the age of fourteen he went to work in the American Sheet and Plate Company's mill. During his twenty years at the plant, he used his spare time to perfect his craft.

That steel rolling mill is preserved today in a 3-by-5-foot working model carved by Warther—a model built with thousands of small, handmade walnut parts. Warther mechanized not only the model's steel rolling equipment, but also many of the workers, including the foreman raising a sandwich to his mouth, a second worker nodding off on the job, and a third "drinking" his lunch by raising a tiny bottle to his lips. An intricate belt-drive system designed by Warther and a sewing machine motor power the model's many moving parts.

Warther's most widely acclaimed carvings, however, are the series he created tracing the history of steam power, particularly his many steam locomotives and trains. Starting with working models of the simplest steam devices dating from 250 B.C., Warther produced models of the various developmental stages of the steam era. By far the most impressive of these are the dozens of steam railroad locomotives on display at the museum, many with hundreds of moving parts.

Warther used walnut for the dark pieces of his models, and, in the early part of his career, pieces of bone for the white pieces. In later years, he could afford ivory and carved entire trains, some with as many as 10,000 parts, from pure white ivory. Warther used arguto, an oil-bearing wood, for the moving parts of his carvings, some of which have run for sixty years without repair.

Of the steam locomotives displayed at Warther's, perhaps the most intriguing is the 8-foot replica of Abraham Lincoln's funeral train. An avid admirer of Lincoln, Warther spent a year at age eighty carving the ebony and ivory locomotive, coal car, funeral car, and passenger cars. Thousands of miniature parts make up the magnificent carving. As an example of the extraordinary detail work done by Warther, the restroom in one of the passenger cars even has a tiny ivory key hanging on a hook on the wall.

Warther's exacting craft demanded fine precision knives and blades, and, not satisfied with those commercially available, he perfected his own custom cutlery. In fact, he supplemented his income by selling this cutlery, a business still operated by his family today. Ernest Warther died at the age of eighty-seven in 1973, leaving his sixty-fourth carving incomplete.

The small original museum behind the present one now houses Mrs. Warther's button collection—over 70,000 buttons, no two alike. Beautiful Swiss-style gardens surround the museums and the Warther home.

Warther's is at 331 Karl Avenue, Dover; (216) 343-7513. Open daily from 9 A.M.–5 P.M., except for major holidays. Admission: adults, $4; children, $2.

Seeking freedom from the new religious tenets in their native Kingdom of Wurttemburg in Germany, 300 men, women, and children known as Separatists, led by Joseph Baumeler, came to 5,500 acres they purchased along the Tuscarawas River, where they established **Zoar Village** in 1817. Two years later, frustrated by their progress to date, the Zoarites abandoned personal property ownership in order to establish a communal system. Under the new system, all property in the village was owned by the Society of Separatists at Zoar, with men and women each given a vote in the election of a board of trustees. The board governed the day-to-day operations of the community, and under this system, with Baumeler remaining as leader of the group, Zoar flourished.

The community established its own farms for food products, a tin shop, a blacksmith shop, two blast furnaces, a bakery, a garden with greenhouse, and a wagon shop. Many of these enterprises produced more goods than needed by the village, with the surplus sold for profit at a store established by the villagers. The Zoarites even landed the contract to build a section of the Ohio and Erie Canal, which passed through their land.

In 1852, the assets of the society were more than a million dollars, and the future appeared bright for this hard-working community. But a year later, Joseph Baumeler was dead, leaving a serious leadership void at Zoar. Baumeler had served as the inspiration of the village, as well as its financial administrator. After his death, Zoar began a gradual decline which persisted for forty years. Finally, in 1898, having lost its competitive edge both in agriculture and in industry, the community disbanded.

Many of the original Zoar buildings have been restored or reconstructed, allowing visitors to better understand the unique experiment that took place here. Inside the Number One House, an audiovisual presentation provides the history of the village. The rooms in this rambling two-story brick building, which once housed the aged and infirm, contain many original furnishings. In the music room, for example, is Peter Bimeler's magnificent hand-built pipe organ. Bimeler was the village miller, and he powered the organ with the mill's water turbine.

The second-floor windows provide a splendid view of the adjacent gardens and greenhouse. A guide at the greenhouse explains the religious significance of the formal gardens, with the large Norway spruce symbolizing Christ and the twelve slip junipers representing the apostles. The greenhouse, constructed in 1835, utilized a unique heating system—charcoal fires burned under the floor and vents funneled the warm air into the greenhouse—allowing the Zoarites to cultivate a wide variety of fruits and vegetables, including tropical fruits. In the Zoar bakery, huge wooden bins stored flour and meal, and the brick oven baked eighty loaves of bread per day.

Other buildings in the village include a tin shop, which has the tools, patterns, and products used and produced by the tinsmith, and the Bimeler House, with its outstanding collection of wool coverlets woven at the community's woolen mill. Knowledgeable guides provide information and answer questions in each building of the village.

Zoar Village is on Rte. 212, Zoar; (216) 874-3211. Open from Memorial Day to Labor Day, Wednesday through Saturday, 9:30 A.M.–4:45 P.M.; Sunday, noon–4:45 P.M. May be open weekends in September and October. Admission: adults, $2; children (ages six to twelve), $1.

The entire town of Zoar is listed on the National Register of Historic Places, and there are a number of antique shops and restaurants in the community. Overnight accommodations are available at Ralph and Judy Kraus's **Cider Mill**. Located right behind the old Zoar Hotel on Second Street, this former barn (built in 1863) has been converted into a shop, a bed and breakfast facility, and the Kraus's residence.

The ground floor houses the shop, with gift and craft items, antiques, and old-fashioned candy, while the two guest rooms are up the spiral staircase on the third floor. Both rooms are furnished with antiques and share a bath. Advance reservations are required.

The Cider Mill is on Second Street, Zoar; (216) 874-3133. Rates are $45 per night, double occupancy (includes breakfast).

Proprietor R.A. Eichel operates **Zoar Tavern**, built in 1831. This structure was once the home of Dr. Clemens Breil, who lived here for many years—in fact, well after the dissolution of the Zoar Society.

Today, Zoar Tavern, refurbished with ceiling fans, hardwood floors, and an old-fashioned jukebox, serves soups, appetizers, salads, and a wide variety of sandwiches. Entrees such as broasted chicken, broiled scrod, and prime rib of beef au jus are also offered, as are a selection of fresh-cut steaks and broiled seafood. Try a hot apple strudel topped with ice cream, French silk chocolate pie, or a hot peanut butter fudge sundae for dessert.

Zoar Tavern is at One Main Street, Zoar; (216) 874-2170. Open daily, 11 A.M.–10 P.M.; Prices: inexpensive to moderate. Visa, MasterCard, and American Express are accepted.

Schoenbrunn Village

Missionary David Zeisberger migrated to the United States in 1737 to work with the American Moravian Church in Bethlehem, Pennsylvania. In 1772, accompanied by a band of Delaware Indians, Zeisberger traveled to the wilderness in Ohio to convert other Indians to Christianity, founding **Schoenbrunn Village**.

The efforts at Schoenbrunn were interrupted by the coming of the Revolutionary War. The village was on the trail between the American outpost at Fort Pitt and the British at Fort Detroit, and neither side trusted the Moravians or their Christian Indians. Harassment eventually forced Zeisberger to abandon Schoenbrunn Village in 1777 and to relocate to a new settlement at nearby Gnadenhutten. Even there, they were not safe. The British arrested Zeisberger and other village leaders and transported them to Detroit for trial on charges of treason. While the leaders were away, American troops, seeking revenge for the death of a settler's wife and children, massacred the Christian Indians at Gnadenhutten, striking them with heavy coopers' mallets.

Schoenbrunn Village today contains eighteen reconstructed rustic log buildings, the original village cemetery, and two and a half acres of planted fields. Log cots with stretched animal skins and a firepit in the center of the floor (with a hole in the roof for smoke to escape) are the only conveniences in some of these cabins. Others feature modest pioneer furnishings such as rough rope spring beds, wooden baby cradles, spinning and flax wheels, and butter churns. Schoenbrunn's settlers constructed Ohio's first schoolhouse, a one-room building completed in 1773. In addition to the log structures, a museum displays Schoenbrunn artifacts excavated from the site, including nails, knives, horseshoes, and chips of cups, jars, and a kettle used at the village more than two hundred years ago.

Schoenbrunn Village is on the southeast edge of New Philadelphia on Rte. 259; (216) 339-3636. Open Memorial Day to Labor Day, Wednesday through Saturday, 9:30 A.M.–4:45 P.M.; Sunday, noon–4:45 P.M. May be open weekends in September and October. Admission: adults, $2; children (ages six to twelve), $1.

For a dramatic presentation of the story of David Zeisberger and the settlement of Schoenbrunn and Gnadenhutten, attend a performance of Paul Green's *Trumpet in the Land*. Staged in a lovely hilltop outdoor amphitheater, this spirited drama uses a mix of song and dance, humor, adventure, and ultimately tragedy to tell of Zeisberger's missionary work in frontier Ohio.

Trumpet in the Land is presented at the Schoenbrunn Amphitheatre on University Drive, just off Rte. 250, New Philadelphia; (216) 339-1132. Performances from late June through Labor Day, Tuesday through Sunday, at 8:30 P.M. Admission: adults, $8 to $8.50; children, $6 to $6.50. Reserved tickets available. MasterCard and Visa are accepted.

Carroll County

Jim and Patty Borton's **Conestoga Farm** offers a relaxing getaway on a 300-acre working farm. Seventeen comfortable cottages face the scenic, tree-lined private lake. For a fixed daily charge, guests are served three meals per day in the rustic dining room, and they can swim in the lake and use the rowboats, canoes, and sailboats.

The eighteen-acre lake also provides anglers with plenty of bass, perch, and bluegill. Other activities included in the fixed rate are tennis (two courts), skeet shooting, hay rides, badminton, volleyball, and corral riding (there is a nominal charge for trail riding on the farm's horses). Farmhands milk Conestoga's dairy cows daily and tend the other livestock—horses, ponies, hogs, sheep, chickens, and rabbits—with guests invited to observe or take part in the farm routine.

The dining hall serves all-you-can-eat meals, with breakfast eggs fresh from the chicken coop and bacon cured right on the farm. Conestoga Farm also dishes up country cooking in a rustic, 100-year-old barn-turned-restaurant called the **Top O'the Farm Restaurant**, so named because of its hilltop location. With the family-style steak and chicken dinners, guests can have all the chicken, salad, vegetables, potatoes, homemade noodles, homemade biscuits, and homemade ice cream they can eat (second steak, half price). Top O'the Farm also offers baked rabbit on Friday nights, and area musicians entertain on both Friday and Saturday evenings. The restaurant is open Friday and Saturday, 5–9 P.M., and Sunday, noon–7 P.M., and prices are moderate.

An old farmhouse at Conestoga has been converted into the Plowshare Ice Cream House and makes the 150 gallons of ice cream consumed each week at the farm and restaurant—ice cream made the old-fashioned rock salt way.

Conestoga Farm is at 1300 Lilly Road Northwest, off Rte. 43 south of Malvern; (216) 863-1606 (local calls) or (800) 547-1548 (toll-free calls from anywhere in Ohio). Open year-round. Rates: adults, $35 per day (children's rates based on age). Daily rate includes a cottage and all meals, plus recreation.

Jefferson County

The **Friends Meeting House**, set in a field in a hilly section of Jefferson County, housed the annual August meeting of 2,000 Ohio and Pennsylvania Quakers for nearly a century. Constructed in 1814, this impressive three-story brick structure measures 92 feet by 60 feet and has walls 2 feet thick.

The Society of Friends relocated an entire meeting from North Carolina to Jefferson County in 1813 and built the meeting house of brick fired right on the site. The interior of the building is one large room, with the original floors, poplar benches, and a large balcony. A massive wooden center divider splits the room—four men in the attic raised and lowered this divider as needed. Men sat on one side of the room during the meetings, women on the other side, and young men and women sat in their respective balconies. The elders and overseers used the facing benches—benches resting on a small platform and facing the congregation. "Strict services" took place here until 1909, with no formal ceremony or music; the group simply meditated in silence until a member felt moved to speak out. The interior of the meeting house is exactly as it was 170 years ago, though it has been more than 70 years since the Quakers last gathered in Jefferson County.

The Friends Meeting House is just off Rte. 150 in Mount Pleasant. Open mid-May to mid-September, Sundays and holidays, 2–5 P.M., or call Mrs. George Welshans, (614) 769-2607 to make an appointment for a tour at other times. Admission: adults, 50¢; children, 25¢.

Guernsey County

Eastern Ohio, western Pennsylvania, and northern West Virginia were once the center of the U.S. glassware industry, and Cambridge, Ohio, was an important city for the glass business. The large Cambridge Glass Company dominated glass production in Guernsey County, opening in the spring of 1902 and shutting down a half century later. While the boom in glassmaking has since passed, the **Degenhart Paperweight and Glass Museum** preserves the heritage of the industry.

By a bequest in her will, Elizabeth Degenhart established the museum. Born in 1889, she had been associated with the glass business most of her life. She went to work at Cambridge Glass at age sixteen and married John Degenhart in 1908. John's father, Andrew, had been a mold maker in several glass factories, and John worked for the Cambridge Glass Company for forty-five years, until his retirement. Even while working at Cambridge, he and Elizabeth would make glass paperweights after hours in their shop at home. John and Elizabeth established the Crystal Art Glass Company, which Elizabeth took over after John's death in 1964.

The museum contains Elizabeth Degenhart's personal collection of paperweights, plus pieces from Cambridge Glass and Crystal Art Glass. Various cut- and blown-glass pieces are displayed, as is an antique glass mold built 150 years ago. An audiovisual presentation explains the history and importance of the glass industry to the area and describes the glassmaking still taking place in Guernsey County.

The Degenhart Paperweight and Glass Museum is on Rte. 22, just west of I-77, Cambridge; (614) 432-2626. The museum is open Monday through Saturday, 10 A.M.–5 P.M.; Sunday, 1–5 P.M., March through December. Closed January and February. Admission: adults, $1.50; children (under eighteen), free.

Just down the street from the museum, **Mosser Glass** offers free tours of their factory to the public. Mosser manufactures glass pitchers, goblets, candleholders, lamps, and animal figures such as frogs, owls, cats, and rabbits.

During the tour, guides explain glassmaking, from heating glass powder to 2,000 degrees in the furnace to forming molten glass in a metal mold. After being pressed in a mold, the shaped glass goes under a flame "glazer," which smooths the surface by reheating the exterior. From there, the molded hot glass cools in a special oven called a Lehr, which uniformly reduces the temperature to prevent shattering. Mosser Glass cranks out 150 pieces of glass per hour.

Mosser Glass is one-half mile west of I-77 on Rte. 22, Cambridge; (614) 439-1827. Tours are given at 8:15, 9:15, 10:15, noon, 1:00, 2:00 and 3:00, Monday through Friday. No tours the last week of June, the first week of July, or Christmas week. No admission charge.

Coshocton County

Roscoe Village served as an important canal port during the Ohio and Erie Canal's boom years in the 1840s and 1850s, with wheat and wool exports traded for coffee and calico. The 308-mile canal extended from Cleveland to Portsmouth, contained 152 locks, and cost $4.7 million to build. Construction of the canal took nine years, ending in 1834 when the canal completed the link between Lake Erie and the Ohio River.

Located near the confluence of the Muskingum, Walhonding, and Tuscarawas rivers, the twenty-five brick and frame buildings in the village ·have been restored to their appearance during the canal's heyday, making Roscoe Village (originally called Caldersburgh) Ohio's only complete canal town restoration.

Six exhibit buildings, a large museum, shops, restaurants, and canalboat rides on the reconstructed *Monticello II* all contribute to the appeal of this unique village. One can purchase tickets to the exhibit buildings scattered throughout the village at the Visitors Center, which also presents a slide program on the history of the canal and village and displays a large, detailed map of the locks and elevation changes along the more than three hundred miles of the canal.

In one of the exhibit buildings, the Toll House, Roscoe's first toll collector, Jacob Welsh, registered incoming canal boats and collected passage fees. Also on display is the compass used in the construction of the canal in the 1820s and 1830s, a canalboat model that travels through a set of double locks, and a working model of a gristmill.

Volunteers weave rugs, wall hangings, and table runners on two antique looms in the Jackson Township Hall, and the village potter throws pots, bowls, and vases in the Craft and Learning Center. Other exhibit buildings include a working blacksmith's shop and the 1840s period home of Dr. Maro Johnson.

Roscoe Village is on Rtes. 16 and 83 near Rte. 36, Coshocton; (614) 622-9310. Open year-round; festivals and special events are April through December. Admission to exhibit buildings: adults, $5; children (eight to eighteen), $2.50.

While in the village, be sure to stop in at **Stewart's Antiques and Collectibles**, where Kenny Stewart has amassed a most extensive collection of . . . well, it's hard to define . . . of *collectibles*! His store window proclaims, "Collectibles today, Antiques tomorrow!" It is not clear which of those two categories best describes his varied inventory.

Kenny's four large rooms are bulging with merchandise, ranging from restored oak iceboxes to old license plates. Glassware, kettles, grinders, scales, and pottery—old coffee tins, biscuit tins, tobacco tins, and political campaign buttons—all fill the shelves and cupboards. And what doesn't fit on a shelf hangs from a hook on the wall or from the ceiling: Kenny does not waste display space. Other items include antique farm implements and kitchen equipment, all types of furniture, and a collection of old detergent boxes and beer cans.

Stewart's Antiques and Collectibles is on Whitewoman Street, in the middle of Roscoe Village, Coshocton. Open 10 A.M.–5 P.M. daily (except when Kenny goes fishing).

The fifty-one room **Roscoe Village Inn** offers fine dining and overnight accommodations in the heart of the village. The inn is a relatively recent addition to this historic community, but its architecture and decor create a traditional flavor.

A pleasant sitting area is typical of the place—high ceilings, warm woods, a vast fireplace, and a grand piano make this a delightful gathering spot. The inn's tavern, with its rough-hewn wood beams and exposed brick walls, is reminiscent of days gone by.

Perhaps most exciting is the excellent kitchen at the Roscoe Village Inn, serving what is without a doubt the most sophisticated food in the area. On my last visit, I thoroughly enjoyed coquilles Saint Jacques mornay—Eastern bay scallops braised in white wine, fresh lemon juice, and mushrooms in a mornay sauce, prepared en casserole with fettucine. Or how about the veal caprice—pan-fried veal cutlets topped with artichoke hearts, Swiss cheese, and a flavorful brown sauce. Fresh seafood du jour, prime rib, chicken, steaks, and lobster tail all await hungry travelers at the Roscoe Village Inn dining room.

The Roscoe Village Inn is located at 200 North Whitewoman Street, Coshocton, (614) 622-2222. Room rates: $63–$68 per night. Meal prices: breakfast and lunch, inexpensive to moderate; dinner, expensive. Visa, MasterCard, and American Express are accepted. Open year-round.

Those fond of guitars, dulcimers, and the like will want to drop in at **Wildwood Stringed Instruments**. Here you'll find antique music makers—a German-built guitar dating from the 1850s, for example—and a complete stock of both new and vintage Martin guitars. Owner and musician Marty Wildwood also sells fine dulcimers made by Bud and Donna Ford of Cripple Creek, Colorado. Harmonicas, mandolins, harpsichords, and miscellaneous supplies round out the inventory here.

Wildwood Stringed Instruments is at 672 Whitewoman Street, on the towpath between Roscoe Village and the canal boat rides; (614) 622-4224. Open Tuesday through Friday, noon–6 P.M.; Saturday and Sunday, 11 A.M.–5 P.M.

The nationally accredited **Johnson-Humrickhouse Museum**, located in Roscoe Village, contains five major galleries, each with its own theme. Indian and Eskimo artifacts, including baskets, pottery, blankets, beadwork, and weapons, are displayed in the Indians of America exhibit. Of particular note are the Eskimo carved ivory tusks and miniature ivory models of kayaks, tools, and dolls. The Joe R. Engle Gallery celebrates "Yesterday in America" with a re-created pioneer home, plus antique tools, farm implements, rare firearms, clocks, pottery, and glassware.

The Oriental Treasures Gallery features splendid carvings in jade, bone, ivory, horn, bamboo, and hardwoods, including an intricate six-panel peach wood screen. One of the museum's most unusual collections is a group of knife rests from all over the world: American glass, French hard porcelain, Japanese enamel, Chinese silver, Zairian ivory, and Burmese teak. The Montgomery Gallery accommodates special events, including national and regional traveling exhibits.

The Johnson-Humrickhouse Museum is on Whitewoman Street, Roscoe Village, Coshocton; (614) 622-8710. Open Tuesday through Sunday, noon–5 P.M. (1–4:30 P.M. during winter months). No admission charge.

Licking County

Approximately 200 million years ago, a layer of hard flint pushed toward the earth's surface in an area known as Flint Ridge. Erosion exposed some of the flint, attracting Indians to the area 8,000 to 10,000 years ago. While the weathered flint was too brittle to be of much value, the Indians discovered a vein of high-quality flint 1 to 10 feet beneath the surface and established crude quarries to extract the material. Using tremendous physical effort and large hammer stones, they pounded bone and wooden wedges into the flint, breaking it into removable chunks.

They used the flint to form arrow and spear points, scrapers, and other tools and to start fires. Because of the demand for flint in prehistoric times, Flint Ridge was considered neutral ground, with members of any tribe allowed to quarry there. White settlers later rediscovered Flint Ridge, using the mineral for buhrstones for gristmills and as roadbed on a nearby section of the National Road.

Today, the **Flint Ridge State Memorial** museum is built around one of the prehistoric Indian quarries, and Indian mannequins stand ready to break up the rock with a stone maul. The museum features an impressive collection of scrapers, drills, hoes, knives, and projectile points. One flint sample contains an excellent impression of a coral animal, created during one of the times when this part of Ohio was under the seas.

A large topographical map illustrates the extent of the ridge in eastern Licking and western Muskingum counties. Other displays include an explanation of the calendar of geological time and descriptions of the various layers of rock in the region, from the surface down to 468 feet underground.

A thick forest of beech, maple, and oak surrounds the museum, and hiking trails pass by old Indian quarries and exposed out-croppings of red, yellow, brown, and creamy flint. One trail takes hikers by two small streams, and abundant wildlife, including deer, squirrels, chipmunks, and birds, can be observed in the park.

Flint Ridge State Memorial is on County Road 668, 3 miles north of Brownsville; (614) 787-2476. The museum is open from Memorial Day through Labor Day, Wednesday through Saturday, 9:30 A.M.–4:45 P.M.; Sunday, noon–4:45 P.M. The museum may be open weekends in September and October. Admission: adults, $1.50; children (ages six to twelve), $1.00.

The 1,150-acre **Dawes Arboretum**, established by Bertie Burr and Beman Gates Dawes in 1929, blends rolling meadows, deep woods, and cultivated gardens. Perhaps the most beautiful area is the Japanese garden designed by noted landscape architect Ma-koto Nakamura. In Nakamura's design, a small lake with islands connected by arched bridges and plantings such as spruce, flow-ering cherries, Japanese yew, and Japanese maple create a tran-quil environment. Another popular area is the cypress swamp, where Southern native bald cypress trees grow and produce "knees."

The holly collection contains 100 distinct types of hollies, and the sugar maples at Dawes provide the sap for the annual pro-duction of maple syrup in the sugar cabin. One section of the arboretum consists of the deciduous climax forest that once blan-keted the entire state of Ohio. In a climax forest, tree seedlings are able to grow in the shade of parent trees, thus reproducing the forest indefinitely in a cycle of growth and regeneration.

One feature of the arboretum can be fully appreciated only from the air—a 2,100-foot-long series of hedges that spell out "Dawes Arboretum." To give perspective on the size of these let-ters, it takes two gardeners a full, eight-hour day to trim the hedges forming each letter.

Other collections at Dawes include oaks, walnuts, birches, red-woods, and dwarf evergreens. In addition to the forests, meadows, and gardens, an 8.5-acre stocked fishing lake can be used by members of the Arboretum. The Visitors Center offers nature exhibits of preserved birds and animals, a bird-watching area, and an indoor beehive which the bees enter from the outside through a clear plastic tube.

Beman and Bertie Dawes moved into the Daweswood House in 1916. Built in the 1840s, this two-story brick home contains antique furnishings and other of the Dawes's possessions, including portraits of famous family members William Dawes, who rode with Paul Revere, and Charles Gates Dawes, who served as vice president in the Coolidge administration. Guides conduct tours of the home daily at 3 P.M. (weekdays only from November through April).

The Dawes Arboretum is on Rte. 13, 5 miles south of Newark; (614) 323-2355. The Visitors Center is open Monday through Friday, 8 A.M.–5 P.M.; Saturday, 9 A.M.–5 P.M., Sunday and holidays, 1–5 P.M. Grounds are open daylight hours. No admission charge except at Daweswood House.

Perhaps Ohio's prettiest small town, Granville dates to its founding in 1805 by settlers from Granville, Massachusetts, and Granby, Connecticut. The nineteenth-century shops and homes in this picture-postcard community are painstakingly maintained. Up on a hill is Denison University, and a more perfect setting for spending college years is difficult to imagine.

In addition to the craft and antique shops, Granville boasts three historic inns, two providing overnight accommodations. Orrin Granger built the **Buxton Inn** (known as the Tavern in Granger's day) in 1812, and the inn has operated continuously since then. The inn housed Granville's first post office and served as a stagecoach stop on the Columbus-Newark line. An addition in 1851 formed the U-shaped structure with center courtyard that exists today. The Buxton is named for one of its more colorful proprietors, Major Buxton, who owned the inn from the close of the Civil War until his death in 1905. The present owners, Mr. and Mrs. Orville Orr, purchased it in 1972 and spent two years researching and completely restoring this outstanding structure, which is now listed on the National Register of Historic Places.

The Buxton serves fine cuisine in tasteful period dining rooms, each unique in mood and ambience. Antiques are proudly displayed throughout the inn, and the brick-floored center courtyard provides a delightful outdoor dining area. Blooming hanging plants in baskets and small potted trees combine with the splash

Buxton Inn

of a nearby fountain and candle-lit tables to make the courtyard a most pleasing place.

For dinner, choose from seafood such as the fresh catch of the day, coquille of seafood cardinal (shrimp, scallops, crabmeat, mushrooms, and mornay) and, one of my favorites, the red snapper with crabmeat au gratin. Other dinner menu options include roast duckling with orange cranberry sauce; chicken victoria with mushrooms, cheese, and ham; medallions of pork fredonia with sauteed pippin apples, and French pepper steak with brandy sauce. Be sure to order the special baked potato, which comes stuffed with cheddar cheese, bacon, chopped onions, sour cream, chives, and butter. The tempting desserts include gingerbread with hot lemon sauce and the chef's double dark chocolate cake.

Luncheon selections such as salads, soups, and sandwiches like the croque monsieur (sauteed ham, Swiss cheese, and fresh mushrooms served with warm syrup or light mustard sauce) join entrees that include quiche, crepes, barbecued ribs, eggs benedict, and seafood Newburg.

Stagecoach drivers once cooked their meals on an open fire in the stone-walled basement of the inn and slept on straw beds around that fire. With its rough beams and imposing stone fireplace, the basement tavern retains the flavor of those early years. The tavern serves a casual menu of sandwiches and appetizers.

While primarily known for fine dining, the Buxton Inn does offer three second-floor guestrooms, all furnished with antiques. Overnight lodging ranges in price from $45 to $55 per night for two people.

The Buxton Inn is at 313 East Broadway, Granville; (614) 587-0001. The inn is open for breakfast, Monday through Friday, 7 A.M.–9 A.M.; Saturday and Sunday, 9 A.M.–11 A.M. Lunch is served Monday through Saturday, 11:30 A.M.–2 P.M.; Sunday, 11 A.M.–2 P.M. Dinner hours are Monday through Thursday, 5:30–9 P.M.; Friday and Saturday, 5:30–10 P.M.; Sunday, noon–8 P.M. The Buxton Tavern is open Monday through Saturday, 5–11 P.M. Prices: lunch, inexpensive to moderate; dinner, expensive. MasterCard and Visa are accepted.

Across the street from the Buxton sits the Tudor-style **Granville Inn**, built in 1924 by the president of the Sunday Creek Coal Company, John Sutphin Jones. With the elegance of an English manor house, the lobby is furnished with splendid antiques and lush oriental rugs. The dining room features high ceilings, ornate brass chandeliers, and sandstone fireplaces. In warm weather, meals are also served out the tall French doors on the flagstone terrace, which is surrounded by a manicured lawn, gardens, and towering trees.

The evening menu at the Granville Inn features a variety of steaks, chops, seafood, chicken, and house specialties such as scallop brochette (skewered scallops adorned with tomatoes, green peppers, onions, and mushroom caps on a bed of wild rice pilaf, seasoned with herb sauce). Another favorite is the baked trout a la mer, which is stuffed with Alaskan crabmeat, shrimp, and herb-seasoned corn bread dressing. All dinners are served with the much-acclaimed fresh raisin bread and honey butter. For a unique appetizer, try the angels on horseback: oysters wrapped in bacon, baked in lemon butter, and served on hot toast triangles.

Luncheon selections include soups, salads, sandwiches, and

entrees such as steaks, chicken vichyssoise, crepes, and the fresh catch of the day. With any meal at the Granville Inn, the house specialty desserts are the English walnut cake and English walnut pie, both served warm.

Individually decorated, the Granville Inn's thirty-one guest rooms have an understated charm and dignity. Prices range from $50 to $55 per night, including a continental breakfast.

The Granville Inn is at 314 East Broadway, Granville; (614) 587-3333. Lunch is served Monday through Saturday, 11:30 A.M.–2:30 P.M. Dinner is Monday through Thursday, 5–9 P.M.; Friday and Saturday, 5–10 P.M. Sunday a buffet is served from 11:30 A.M.–2:30 P.M. Prices: lunch, inexpensive to moderate; dinner, moderate to expensive. MasterCard, Visa, and American Express are accepted.

Granville's most elegant dining takes place 2 miles south of the central business district in a splendid pale yellow former mansion, **Bryn Mawr**. The name Bryn Mawr translates from Welch as "big hill," a name the man who built this estate, Elias Fassett, chose. Fassett, who was president of the Central Ohio Railroad, constructed the stately home, with its towering Ionic columns, on the hillside in 1850. After his death, the property changed hands frequently and was finally acquired by its present owners, who opened it as a restaurant in 1974.

Inside the impressive entryway, a large grandfather clock stands solemnly in the center hall. The four first-floor dining rooms each exude a tasteful refinement, from the luxurious Italian marble fireplace, crystal chandelier, and potted plants in the drawing room, to the bay windows, French doors, and Williamsburg chandeliers in the main dining room. The basement dining area, with its burning candles and fireplaces and exposed brick and stone, is slightly less formal, but has the same integrity as the upstairs. The pianist at the baby grand sets the mood with arrangements of Gershwin, Cole Porter, Chopin, and Rodgers and Hammerstein.

Identical menus are served upstairs and in the basement, with creative entrees such as stuffed beef tenderloin (a personal favorite with its Swiss cheese, smoked ham, crabmeat, and asparagus set in a choice filet), scallops Florentine, and bali hai (a Polynesian-style breast of chicken with sweet and sour ribs). Other entree options include choice cuts of steak, the seafood or quiche of the day, plus chicken and crab Bryn Mawr (topped with cream sauce, toasted almonds, and snow peas). Dinner is served with delicious homemade soups, fresh breads, and the popular hot cinnamon rolls. Desserts include a variety of bartender pies, with different selections offered nightly.

Bryn Mawr lunches consist of quiche, salads, sandwiches, homemade chicken pot pie, and an appealing beef tenderloin, which contains bits of beef and fresh mushrooms in a brown sauce with sour cream over buttered broad noodles. Lunch is also served on the terrace, weather permitting.

Bryn Mawr is on Rte. 37, 2 miles south of Granville; (614) 587-4000. Lunch is served Monday through Friday, 11:30 A.M.–1:30 P.M. Dinner is Monday through Thursday, 5:30–9:30 P.M.; Friday and Saturday, 5:30–10 P.M. The popular Sunday brunch has two seatings, one at 11 A.M., the other at 12:30 P.M., with reservations suggested. Sunday dinner is served from 4 to 7 P.M. Prices: lunch, inexpensive to moderate; dinner, moderate to expensive. Master-Card and Visa are accepted.

A devastating fire at **Ye Olde Mill** near Utica in April, 1986, completely destroyed the 100-year-old structure. Only the 18-foot, 2,000-pound waterwheel and the quarry stone survived the blaze.

But the Velvet Ice Cream Company, which operates the mill and has its headquarters next door, set about building a new Ye Olde Mill of rough-sawed oak and poplar. And this new building is open for business, selling country crafts, serving items from a short-order menu and, not surprisingly, Velvet Ice Cream.

The 1870-vintage building destroyed by fire was not the first mill on this site—a sawmill was erected here in 1817, and a larger one went up in 1827. You can find out about this, and more, at the museum of milling history and ice cream recently added to Ye Olde Mill.

Once you've picked up a cone full of your favorite ice cream flavor, step outside to the parklike picnic area. Relax at the picnic tables while watching the ducks frolic in a picturesque pond.

Ye Olde Mill is 10 miles north of Newark on Rte. 13, Utica; (614) 892-3921. Open daily, May 15 through October, Monday through Saturday, 11 A.M.–9 P.M.; Sunday, noon–9 P.M.

Muskingum County

Imports dominate the basket industry in the United States to-day, but one Ohio family continues three generations of hand-crafted basket making. Before the turn of the century, John

Longaberger began weaving baskets for his neighbors and local potteries, which used them for storing and shipping their fragile products. John's son J. W. Longaberger expanded the business after World War I and taught his twelve children the art of basket making in the evening, after he worked a full day at a nearby paper mill. But over the years, inexpensive cardboard, plastic, and metal containers drastically reduced the industrial demand for Longaberger's baskets, and production slowed to a trickle.

In the 1970s, however, J.W.'s son Dave, with his father's help, revived the business after becoming convinced a new market existed for good quality, handmade baskets. The 350 weavers producing nearly seven thousand baskets per day at the **Longaberger Basket Company** are proof of Dave's acumen. From a roped-off viewing area, visitors watch the weavers work hard maple bands around a Longaberger mold. Hard maple is best for basket weaving because it is very smooth and pliable, not splintery. Most of the maple used here originates in Ohio, though some comes from Pennsylvania and West Virginia. All baskets use oak handles, many are stained in a popular walnut finish, and, as an example of the emphasis on quality control in the plant, each weaver initials and dates each basket.

Commissioned sales representatives sell the handcrafted Longaberger baskets at in-home basket parties throughout the United States.

The Longaberger Basket Company is at 95 North Chestnut, Dresden; (614) 754-2031.

As the name indicates, the **National Road–Zane Grey Museum** actually houses two museums—one presenting the story of the building of the National Road connecting the western territories with the original eastern states, and the other commemorating author Zane Grey, the Zanesville, Ohio, native known through his travels and writing as the "High Priest of the Outdoors."

Built in stages from 1811 to 1838, the National Road stretched from Cumberland, Maryland, to Vandalia, Illinois. George Washington originally conceived the idea of constructing a road into the new nation's western lands, and the ninth Congress of the United States approved funds for this first federally supported road in 1806.

Workers earned a dollar per day to clear a 66-foot-wide path and to build a 30-foot-wide roadbed of broken stone using handtools, mules, oxen, and horses. The National Road was vital to the development of the frontier—as each section of the road opened, settlers loaded their Conestoga wagons and headed west.

The museum displays horse-drawn carts, buggies, and wagons (including a Conestoga wagon), plus antique bicycles and automobiles—all methods of transportation utilized on the National Road (which eventually became U.S. 40 and reached all the way to California). A 136-foot diorama depicts the chronology of the road, from its construction and use by early settlers moving west, to farmers herding their livestock on the road and the road's revival after the invention of the bicycle and automobile. Other exhibits include photographs of sections of the road under construction and fully equipped interiors of blacksmith and wheelwright shops.

Author Zane Grey, born in 1875, acquired his passion for hunting and fishing around Dillon Falls, near his home in Zanesville. Grey attended dental school at the University of Pennsylvania, where he also played on the college baseball team. But Grey abandoned his dental career to write, achieving national prominence with his sixty Western novels, many of which were later filmed as motion pictures. He used the money from his books and movies to finance his worldwide fishing trips and big game hunting expeditions.

The museum displays many of Zane Grey's books, magazine articles, and posters from his motion pictures, plus the lures and hunting rifles used on Grey's travels. There is also a complete replica of the study he added to his Altadena, California, home, where he penned many of his works.

The National Road–Zane Grey Museum is at the Norwich exit of I-70, 10 miles east of Zanesville; (614) 872-3143. Open from March through November, Wednesday through Saturday, 9:30 A.M.–5 P.M.; Sunday, noon–5 P.M. This museum is also open Monday and Tuesday, 9:30 A.M.–5 P.M., May through September. Admission: adults, $2; children, $1.

The four Ransbottom brothers—Frank, Ed, Johnie, and Mort—purchased the Oval Ware and Brick Company in 1900, each bringing expertise in a particular phase of the pottery business. Ed and Mort had held supervisory positions at the nationally respected Roseville Pottery Company; Frank was a successful pottery wholesaler, and Johnie turned and jiggered pottery at numerous local plants.

Their company, Ransbottom Brothers Pottery Company, grew quickly. By 1906 the firm was a leading producer of stoneware jars, manufacturing 12,000 gallons of stoneware per day. Chang-ing markets in the 1920s caused the demand for stoneware jars to decline, so the Ransbottoms merged with the Robinson Clay Product Company and shifted their production to gardenware such as bird baths, planting tubs, jardinieres, pots, vases, urns, and strawberry jars. These products have remained the mainstay of the company's line to this day.

The **Robinson-Ransbottom Pottery Company** offers free, self-guided tours of its large factory. Following a printed guide sheet, visitors observe each step of the pottery-making process. The locally dug clay travels by conveyor to the pug mill to be mixed, and the prepared clay is then distributed throughout the plant for production. Sharp-bladed machines slice the clay into precise lengths, and molds press the clay into the desired shape. After drying, the pottery is fired in either a round or continuous kiln.

The round brick kilns, built at the turn of the century, each hold approximately thirty tons of pottery (20,000 pieces); it takes seven working days to load, fire, and unload each of the two round kilns. In the continuous kilns, the pottery is fired while slowly traveling from one end to the other. Since both types of kilns burn natural gas to supply the needed heat, the tempera-tures in this part of the factory can be quite high. Artist Sally Guy hand paints some of the larger vases, and pottery from the fac-tory can be purchased at the adjacent Pot Shop.

The Robinson-Ransbottom Pottery Company is off Rte. 93, 1 mile north of Roseville in Ironspot; (614) 697-7355. Factory tours are Monday through Friday, 8:15 A.M.–2:15 P.M. No admission charge.

Off the Beaten Path
in Southeast Ohio

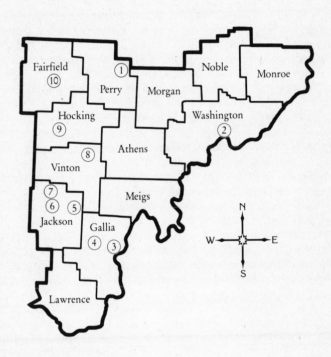

1. Ohio Ceramics Center
2. Marietta
3. Our House Museum
4. Bob Evans Farm
5. Buckeye Furnace
6. Lake Katharine
7. Leo Petroglyph
8. Lake Hope State Park
9. Hocking Hills
10. Georgian/R.J. Pitcher Inn

Southeast Ohio

Perry County

Abundant clay deposits in eastern Ohio, particularly in Perry and Muskingum counties, encouraged the manufacture of pottery and ceramic wares in this section of the state. Pottery production in these counties dates to the early nineteenth century, and twenty-two major pottery companies once generated clay products in the area. Only eight of those firms remain in business, but the **Ohio Ceramics Center** preserves the history of the industry and displays samples of the diverse output of those factories.

Set on a hilltop in a cluster of trees, the center consists of five open-air exhibit buildings. Guides provide the background and explain the processes used to produce the assortment of vases, jugs, pots, and pitchers, plus plates, saucers, and other dinnerware—each unique in shape, color, and clay mixture. Some of the older pieces include stoneware jugs and jars from the 1850s, and the even older earthenware, which was made from very soft red clay.

The yellowware, so named because of its yellow hue, came from the East Liverpool, Ohio, area, as did the most unusual brown rockingham pottery. Rockingham (also manufactured in Vermont and Great Britain) can be easily identified by the pitcher handles shaped as a dog—a dog that appears to be looking into the pitcher. The guides also explain the obvious similarity in style of pieces from different companies—the firms frequently hired employees away from one another, and these employees often brought to their new employer the techniques and processes used by competitors.

Modern pottery displays include samples of dinnerware and decorative pottery currently in production at the remaining local companies. The museum also exhibits pottery-making equipment such as molds and old potters' wheels, plus examples of industrial uses of ceramics—drain tubes, shingles, chimney liners, and even filters for air-pollution devices. A resident potter demonstrates the craft of hand-throwing vases, bowls, and jugs and describes glazing and finishing procedures. Two large shelter houses recently have been added at the center, where antique pottery is sold on special occasions, the proceeds used to help support this facility.

The Ohio Ceramics Center is on Rte. 93 between Roseville and Crooksville; (614) 697-7021. The center is open summer months (season may be extended), Wednesday through Saturday, 10 A.M.– 5 P.M.; Sunday, noon–5 P.M. Admission: $1 for everyone over age twelve.

Washington County

At the conclusion of the Revolutionary War, Congress passed the "Ordinance of 1787" which opened up new land west and north of the Ohio River for settlement. A group of soldiers and officers from the Revolutionary conflict, along with other New Englanders, formed the Ohio Company of Associates to settle in this frontier territory. On April 7, 1788, a party of forty-eight men on a crude barge followed the Ohio River to the Muskingum River, arriving at today's location of **Marietta**, Ohio. By July of that year, Governor Arthur St. Clair had established the first civil government west of the Allegheny Mountains in Marietta, with the settlement destined to be Ohio's first city and gateway to the Northwest Territory (Ohio, Michigan, Indiana, Illinois, Wisconsin, and part of Minnesota). The city was named for Queen Marie Antoinette, in gratitude for the support France had provided the colonies during the war with the British.

Rufus Putnam, a general under Washington during the Revolution, led that forty-eight–man party in April, 1788, and supervised the construction of a walled fortification with four blockhouses to discourage Indian attacks. Putnam's home was part of that fortification and still exists today, completely enclosed in the **Campus Martius Museum**. Putnam coined the name Campus Martius, which means "field of wars," but the Treaty of Greene Ville in 1795 virtually ended hostilities in the region.

Putnam's 200-year-old home rests on its original foundation and contains furnishings from the Putnam family. Guides describe the hardships of early pioneer life and explain the use of the various kitchen and household implements on display.

The museum also exhibits hundreds of items from Marietta's early days, such as the compasses and surveyors' chains used to plat the city. Other collections include Dr. John Cotton's surgical equipment (he practiced medicine in Marietta from 1815 to

1847), antique musical instruments, and a very unusual studio portrait camera from the early 1900s.

One entire gallery contains nineteenth-century ladies' apparel—the lavish gowns and dresses worn during that era. An outdoor patio features an outstanding assortment of Franklin stoves, a water pumper (c. 1853) used to fight fires, and the enormous pilot wheel from the stern-wheel towboat *J.C. Risher*, which worked the Ohio River from 1873 until it sank in 1919. A military display includes the sword used by General Putnam during the Revolutionary War (he later gave this sword to George Washington), old rifles and muskets used by early settlers in the area, uniforms and dress swords from the War of 1812, and a Confederate flag captured at the Civil War battle of Chancellorsville, plus uniforms, saddlebags, and a fife and drum used by Civil War soldiers.

The Campus Martius Museum is at the corner of Washington (Rte. 7) and Second streets, Marietta; (614) 373-3750. The museum is open from March through November, Wednesday through Saturday, 9:30 A.M.–5 P.M.; Sunday, noon–5 P.M. Also open Mondays and Tuesdays, 9:30 A.M.–5 P.M., May through September. Admission: adults, $2; children (ages six to twelve), $1.

With their tall smokestacks puffing black ash and their paddleboards splashing the waters of the Ohio and Muskingum rivers, the great stern-wheelers plied these waterways carrying freight and passengers during the nineteenth century. Marietta was once a thriving port; its history is interwoven with that of the rivers and the steamboat era.

The **Ohio River Museum** stands on the bank of the Muskingum River, just down the street from Campus Martius. The museum actually consists of four separate buildings connected with covered outdoor walkways. One building's maps, models, and illustrations trace the origins of the Ohio River—the role of glaciers in its development and the natural history of the region. A half-hour multimedia presentation gives the river's more recent past from its early exploration to modern-day commercial and recreational usage.

The most popular building features dozens of detailed models of stern-wheeled paddleboats, with the statistics and a narrative of each vessel provided, plus other riverboat memorabilia such as newspaper clippings, passenger tickets, bills of lading, and stern-wheeler travel brochures. The museum also houses a fine collection of steam whistles and a complete set of woodworking tools used for shipbuilding.

The major outdoor attraction at the Ohio River Museum—the 175-foot, 342-ton *W.P. Snyder, Jr.*—was the last steam-powered stern-wheeled towboat to operate in America. It is now permanently docked on the Muskingum River right behind the museum; visitors walk the gangplank to explore this proud vessel from engine room to pilot house. Built in 1918, the *W.P. Snyder, Jr.* plied America's rivers until 1955.

Other outdoor exhibits include a skiff built in 1885, believed to be the oldest such boat in the inland lakes region, which was used during one of the many floods that rampaged in Marietta prior to the installation of flood-control dams. The museum also has a replica of an early flatboat, the flat-bottomed, square-cornered boats used to float heavy cargoes downstream. Propelled only by the river's current, these boats were dismantled (their wood sold for construction projects) upon arriving at their destination.

The Ohio River Museum is at the corner of Front and Saint Clair streets, Marietta; (614) 373-3717. Open March through November, Wednesday through Saturday, 9:30 A.M.–5 P.M.; Sunday, noon–5 P.M. The museum is also open Mondays and Tuesdays, 9:30 A.M.–5 P.M., May through September. Admission: adults, $2; children (ages six to twelve), $1.

Given the importance of stern wheelers to Marietta's past, it seems only proper to survey the city and surrounding area from aboard one—the **Valley Gem**, which docks adjacent to the Ohio River Museum. Captain James E. Sands pilots this ninety-eight–passenger excursion vessel down the Muskingum and Ohio rivers on fifty-minute cruises.

During the trips, Captain Sands points out the historic places of interest along the shoreline, including the location of Fort Harmar (built in 1785) and the Showboat Becky Thatcher, a popular restaurant which presents melodrama theater during summer months. Large stone blocks spelling "Marietta" mark the landing once used by arriving steamboats, and this landing is now the site of the annual stern-wheeler festival. Graceful stern-wheelers come from all parts of the inland waterway system to compete in races and generally show off during this annual weekend of activities.

The *Valley Gem* departs from the landing under the Washington Street Bridge at Front Street, Marietta; (614) 373-7862. During the summer, she sails Tuesday through Sunday at 1, 2, 3, 4, and 5 P.M. In April, May, and September, river trips depart on weekends and holidays at 1, 2, 3, and 4 P.M. Rates: adults, $3, children, $2.

Four-hour fall foliage tours leave the landing on Saturdays and Sundays, in October at 9 A.M. and 1 P.M. Rates: adults, $8; children, $4. (Reservations are recommended for foliage tours.)

If lunch or dinner is the next priority after your riverboat ride, try the **Betsey Mills Club Dining Room**. A favorite place with local people, this women's club was founded by Betsey Gates Mills in 1911 under the name Girls' Monday Club. The club evolved from a sewing class started by Mrs. Mills in 1898 and later offered instruction in the "household sciences and arts" as well as involvement in social work.

In 1916, Betsey Mills and her husband, W. W. Mills, purchased the home where she was born at the corner of Putnam and Fourth streets and donated it to the club. Not only was the 1830s structure the birthplace of Mrs. Mills, but her nephew, Charles G. Dawes, was also born there. Dawes served as vice president of the United States under Calvin Coolidge from 1925 to 1929, authored the Dawes Plan for the war reparations after World War I, and was awarded the Nobel Peace Prize.

After Mrs. Mills' death, Mr. Mills expanded the club, joining two adjacent buildings under one roof. Today, the club continues to provide services for the girls and women of Marietta, including the rental of 15 inexpensive rooms to young working women in the area, organizations for junior high and high school girls, and instruction in everything from art to sports.

The dining rooms in the club are open to the public, each tastefully decorated with cheerful wallpapers and drapes and plenty of potted plants. Looking out the windows, you have a view of the brick patios, well-maintained gardens and wrought-iron fences and gates, which surround this historic two-story building.

With a reputation for quality food at reasonable prices, the Betsey Mills Club serves luncheon entrees such as french toast and sausage, quiche and liver and onions, plus a choice of sandwiches (reubens, stacked steak on a kaiser roll and a dozen others), with fresh fruit salad served in season. The generous dinners at the club include baked stuffed pork chops, steak in brown gravy, cod filet almondine and scalloped chicken. These include a choice of salad and two vegetables.

The Betsey Mills Club Dining Room is at the corner of Fourth and Putnam streets, Marietta; (614) 373-3804. The club offers lunch Monday through Saturday, 11 A.M.–2 P.M.; and dinner Monday through Saturday, 5–8 P.M.; Sunday, 11:30 A.M.–2:30 P.M.

Prices: lunch, inexpensive; dinner, moderate. MasterCard and Visa are accepted.

After your meal, be sure to take a walking or driving tour of Marietta's stately residential neighborhoods. The city contains hundreds of nineteenth-century homes, many on charming brick streets.

For overnight accommodations, the **Lafayette Hotel** is at the landing where steamboats once unloaded their passengers and cargoes on cruises between Pittsburgh and Cincinnati. Nautical memorabilia decorate the lobby, restaurants, and lounge in this building (1918), including brass pilot instruments, a pilot wheel, and paintings and photographs of the stern-wheelers that once prowled the nation's rivers.

The hotel's 91 guest rooms feature knotty wood paneling, and three even offer private balconies facing the river. Special Marietta lodging and entertainment packages are also available.

The Lafayette Hotel is at the corner of Front and Greene streets, Marietta; (800) 331-9337 (Ohio), (800) 331-9336 (out of state), (614) 373-5522. Rates: $40 to $75 night. MasterCard, Visa and American Express are accepted.

Gallia County

The settlement of Gallipolis resulted directly from what had to be one of the first land speculation schemes in the history of the United States. A congressman and his business associates received a congressional grant for 3.5 million acres in southern Ohio. These investors planned to secure the funds to pay for this land by reselling large tracts to Europeans. They formed the Scioto Company and dispatched a sales representative to France, who easily sold tracts to 500 upper-class French citizens ready to leave the turmoil in their country. These 500 men, women and children set sail for America in 1790, but by the time they arrived in the New World, the Scioto Company had failed, leaving the immigrants without their property.

After negotiations with Congress, the French were given frontier land on the Ohio River. Since these immigrants were largely noblemen, professionals and artisans, pioneer life quickly took its toll. Half of the party deserted the frontier during the first two years for "more civilized" areas.

But those remaining in what is today Gallipolis endured, and the town's strategic location on the river spurred its growth. In 1819, Henry Cushing constructed a tavern and inn, and that two-story building still exists, now a museum known as **Our House**.

The doors, floors—even the lock on the front door at Our House—are all original. A grandfather clock built in 1780 still keeps time, and the museum contains Chippendale and Hepplewhite furnishings that belonged to early Gallipolis settlers. In the dining room, for example, is a magnificent cherry dining room table set with delicate French plates and serving trays. The second-floor ballroom still has the original carved wooden chandeliers.

The name Our House comes from the sales pitch its owner, Henry Cushing, would give when he met boats arriving at the docks. To keep the newcomers from going to the other inn in town, he would tell them, "Come to our house." The inn's most famous guest was the French general and statesman Marquis de Lafayette. Lafayette, after his first trip to the colonies in 1777 to fight with the Americans against the British, returned to France and convinced his countrymen to enter the war against England. America never forgot Lafayette's aid during the Revolution, and in 1825 he made a triumphant return to the United States, which included a two-and-a-half-hour visit to Gallipolis and Our House on May 22. The coat he wore and one of the violins used to entertain him are displayed at the museum.

Another important Frenchman planned to come to Gallipolis with the original 500 settlers but at the last minute let his fiancee go without him. Had he made the trip to America, history would have been dramatically altered. His name was Napoleon Bonaparte; his fiancee's portrait hangs above a fireplace at Our House.

Our House is at 434 First Avenue, Gallipolis; (614) 446-0586. The museum is open Wednesday through Friday, 9:30 A.M.–5 P.M.; Saturday, 9 A.M.–5 P.M.; Sunday, 1–5 P.M. No admission charge, but donations are appreciated.

Bob Evans has made his mark in two related businesses—as a manufacturer and distributor of his country sausage and as the proprietor of the Bob Evans Restaurants. After World War II, Evans opened a twelve-stool restaurant near Gallipolis. Not satisfied with the sausage available commercially, he started making his own. This blossomed into Bob Evans's sausage business, and he devoted more and more of his time and energy to it. Once Bob Evans Sausage was firmly established in the marketplace, he once again concentrated on the restaurant business, opening a second location in 1962 and coordinating a major expansion in the late 1960s. Today, Bob Evans Sausage is sold in twenty states, and more than one-hundred and eighty restaurants serve customers throughout the Midwest.

The 1,100-acre **Bob Evans Farm** consists of fields, woodlands, and scenic Raccoon Creek. Evans purchased the farm in 1953, living there with his family until 1971. He maintains the company's offices in the farmhouse, but the rest of the acreage now is open to the public. Free fifty-minute wagon tours of the property take place on the hour, and local artists display (and sell) handmade gifts such as wood carvings, placemats, and jewelry in the Craft Barn.

Throughout the year, the farm hosts special events, including canoe races, dulcimer festivals, antique car shows, and fairs. The most popular is the annual International Chicken Flying Meet. Chickens, not known for their aeronautic prowess, are motivated into the air with a bathroom plunger from the special mailbox launching platforms at the flying field in a race for distance. Some fly forward, some backward or sideways, some not at all, but the crowd cheers them on nonetheless.

The farm offers guided horseback rides on its many bridle trails for $7 per hour. Overnight trail rides leave the stable three nights each week during the summer months and on Saturday nights in September. After a two-and-a-half-hour ride to the campsite, guides serve a campfire supper (including—what else?—Bob Evans sausage). After a night outdoors and a hearty breakfast, riders saddle up and return to the stables. For $40 per person, the farm furnishes horses, meals, tents, and shelters—you just bring your clothing, sleeping bag, or bed roll and perhaps some insect repellent. These popular overnights fill quickly, so reservations are a must.

The farm's canoe livery rents canoes and equipment for trips down Raccoon Creek ranging from one hour to a wilderness overnight trip. The picturesque creek takes canoeists past old gristmills and the cave Daniel Boone and two companions used during the winters of 1791 and 1792 while hunting and trapping beaver. Artifacts discovered in this 95-by-60-foot cave indicate prehistoric Indians took shelter here nearly 5,000 years ago. Canoe rentals range in price from $8.50 per canoe for the shorter trips to $20 for longer excursions. The canoeing season extends from April through October, weekends 8:30 A.M.–5:00 P.M. in the

69

spring and fall, and daily those same hours during summer months.

Bob Evans Farm is on Rte. 35, 1 mile east of Rio Grande; (614) 245-5305. The farm is open weekends in April, May, September, and October and daily in the summer, 9 A.M.–5 P.M. No admission charge.

Jackson County

The 100-mile-long, 30-mile-wide belt of southern Ohio and northern Kentucky known as the Hanging Rock Iron Region once produced the iron demanded by the booming industrial revolution. Eighty charcoal furnaces operated in this region from 1818 to 1916, furnishing iron ingots used to manufacture railroad and farm equipment, heavy machinery—even the cannons and gunboats used in the Civil War. Abundant quantities of the iron ore, limestone, and timber needed for iron production caused the proliferation of furnaces in the region, and furnace communities sprang up near these facilities.

While many of the region's sandstone stacks today stand in silent memory of this once vital industry, at **Buckeye Furnace**, Ohio's only restored charcoal furnace, all buildings have been reconstructed. Visitors learn the history of the Hanging Rock region and the basics of iron making by reading the many signs along Buckeye's self-guided tour.

The furnace was built into a hillside, and the raw materials (iron ore, limestone, and charcoal) were brought by wagon to the top of the hill, where the charcoal was stored under a stock shed to keep it dry, and the limestone and ore were graded and sorted. (The charcoal was produced at a separate location by slowly burning timber under mounds of earth.) Laborers mixed and poured enormous quantities of these materials into the top of the furnace: in a twelve-hour shift, they would measure and load 57,000 pounds of ore, 1,900 pounds of limestone, and 800 bushels of charcoal. As the charcoal burned, temperatures in the furnace reached 600 degrees, causing the impurities in the iron ore to mix with the limestone, forming a waste product called slag. Since molten iron is heavier than slag, the iron could be removed from the bottom of the furnace by opening a stone dam at its base. The liquid iron flowed into sand molds known as pigs. The process of loading raw materials (the "burden") and drawing off the slag and molten iron was continuous—the furnaces operated twenty-four hours a day.

Down the hill from the stock shed and loading area, the Buckeye Furnace general store contains merchandise typical of the nineteenth century. The companies often paid the laborers in scrip, rather than currency, which could only be used at the company store or to pay for company lodging. As a result, some workers were continually in debt to their employers.

The discovery of richer and more easily transported Lake Superior iron ore caused the decline of the Hanging Rock Iron Region. Buckeye Furnace shut down for the last time in 1894, closing a chapter in the state's industrial history.

Buckeye Furnace is off Rte. 124, 10 miles east of Jackson; (614) 384-3537. Open Memorial Day to Labor Day, Wednesday through Saturday, 9:30 A.M.–5 P.M.; Sunday, noon–5 P.M. (May be open on weekends in September and October.) Admission: adults, $2; children (ages six to twelve), $1.

Northwest of Jackson, the **Lake Katharine State Nature Preserve** contains 1,400 breathtaking acres of rolling wooded hills, dense vegetation, and a cool, clear lake. Stop by the manager's office for maps of the main hiking trails (which are located across the lake from the office) and walk down the path near the office for your first view of tranquil Lake Katharine.

It's a scenic drive to the parking area adjacent to the start of the three main trails on the east side of the lake. The Calico Bush Trail, a favorite in late April and May with wildflower lovers, leads hikers past abundant calico bush (mountain laurel) in full bloom on and between the exposed sandstone formations.

The Pine Ridge Trail crosses Rock Run, a gurgling stream that supplies Lake Katharine's sparkling water, and follows the lakeshore. This 2-mile trail then rises through a ridge of pines to a spectacular overlook.

Ohio's Youth Conservation Corps completed the preserve's newest and most demanding trail in 1979—Salt Creek Trail. Traveling 2 miles of steep hills, wooded ravines, cliffs, and creeks, hikers pass abandoned drift mines, early Indian work sites, and burial pits.

Visitors to this pristine preserve frequently spot varied wildlife, including wild turkey and deer, and occasionally a bobcat or king snake. Because this is a nature preserve, no bank fishing, swimming, or picnicking is allowed, and non-motorized watercraft are permitted on the winding lake by written permit only, with a maximum of five boats allowed per day.

Lake Katharine State Nature Preserve is 3 miles northwest of Jackson, off Rte. 35 on County Road 59; (614) 286-2487. Open daylight hours, no admission charge.

Just north of Lake Katharine, under a protective roof, rests a large slab of black hand sandstone (see Hocking County) with some remarkable Indian carvings—the **Leo Petroglyph**. Probably carved by the Fort Ancient Indians more than seven-hundred years ago, the petroglyph has forty different carved figures, with a fish, a bird, and three human feet plainly visible. The most intriguing carving shows an Indian wearing an elaborate headdress. Nature trails penetrate the deep woods and skirt the upper cliffs of the gorges and forests surrounding the petroglyph.

The Leo Petroglyph is on County Road 28, off Rte. 35, 4 miles northwest of Jackson. Open daylight hours, no admission charge.

Vinton County

Ohio's state parks offer hundreds of cabins throughout the state, most of them the modern, two-bedroom deluxe model. For those seeking more rustic and less expensive lodging, **Lake Hope State Park** provides the widest selection in types of cabins in the state park system. In addition to deluxe cabins, Lake Hope has twenty-one standard cabins with wood-burning fireplaces. These cabins, available April through October, accommodate up to six people in four rooms and contain complete kitchens. A third type, the sleeping cabins, have one to four bedrooms, fireplaces, and refrigerators, but no cooking facilities. As with the modern deluxe cabins, the sleeping cabins are available year-round.

The 3,000-acre park includes 120-acre Lake Hope, with its large beach and swimming area, in a heavily wooded section of Vinton County. The park's dining lodge serves meals from May through October, and the park has miles of hiking trails, as does the adjacent state forest. Lake Hope State Park also contains the remains of an old charcoal furnace—Hope Furnace.

Lake Hope State Park is on Rte. 278, 5 miles north of Zaleski; (614) 596-5253. Deluxe cabins range in price from $48 per day to $198 per week; standard cabins, $36 per day to $156 per week; sleeping cabins, $32 to $50 per day, $140 to $200 per week.

Hocking County

Southeast Ohio contains thousands of acres of rugged, hilly countryside covered with thick forests, but the most geologically intriguing area may be the 10,000-acre **Hocking Hills State Park and Forest**. Steep hills, deciduous and evergreen forests, caves, rivers, waterfalls, and abundant plant and animal life provide outstanding recreational opportunities.

A warm, shallow ocean covered Ohio some three-hundred million years ago and deposited the bedrock of shale and black hand sandstone found in the area. Black hand sandstone is so named because of a large black hand drawn on a slab of the stone near Newark. Probably drawn by Indians, the hand may have served as a marker pointing the way to the outcroppings of flint found at Flint Ridge.

Though primitive man may have used the caves, recesses, and cliffs in the Hocking Hills for shelter as long as 7,000 years ago, pottery fragments confirm the Adena Indians lived here from the time of Christ to A.D. 800. White settlers did not discover the lush forests and flowing streams in these hills until the 1790s.

Old Man's Cave, one of the six major formations in the park, so awed Richard Rowe with its natural beauty in the late 1800s that he decided to live at the cave as a hermit for the rest of his days. Rowe was the "old man" for whom this cave is named. A deep gorge runs along the cave, which is actually a major recess in the sandstone cliff, and water flowing through the bottom of the gorge is hurled over two waterfalls and into the Devil's Bathtub, a large pothole formed in the sandstone by swirling rock and gravel in the stream water. Hiking trails follow the ridges on both sides of the gorge, and a third snakes through the hemlocks, beeches, yews, and firs at the bottom of the gorge.

Decades of erosion have created another spectacular sandstone formation called Ash Cave, a 700-foot horseshoe-shaped rock ledge which forms a recess 100 feet deep. Mounds of ash found here by early settlers indicated that this large rock roof was a popular camping site for Indians. Hiking trails run along both ridges and the floor of the gorge, past the 90-foot waterfall.

The Rock House, a massive cavern completely enclosed by rock except for the open "windows," is the most cavelike formation in the park—certainly more so than Ash Cave or Old Man's Cave—yet of the three it is the only one not named a cave. Another misnomer is nearby Cedar Falls, a waterfall named by pioneers who mistakenly identified the dense forest as cedar, when, in fact, it is hemlock.

In addition to the six major formations in the park, hiking trails explore thousands of acres in the thickly wooded state forest. The park has forty deluxe cabins in a secluded, peaceful setting and a dining lodge with outdoor swimming pool. The cabins are available year-round, but are rented only for full weeks during summer months, with rates ranging from $48 per day to $198 per week. The dining lodge serves meals from March through November. Other park features include campsites, a seventeen-acre fishing lake, and a summer naturalist program, plus picnic tables, barbecue grills, and shelters scattered throughout the area.

Hocking Hills State Park is 14 miles west of Logan, on Rte. 664; (614) 385-6841, 385-6165.

It took more time and money than they ever imagined, but Anne Castle and friends finally have created the **Inn at Cedar Falls**. Situated on a hillside meadow, surrounded on three sides by the Hocking Hills State Park, the inn represents two and a half years of work and an investment of a half million dollars.

Anne and crew first removed shingle and plaster from an 1850s-vintage farmhouse, purchased from an eighty-six-year-old woman who was born here, to reveal its original log and mud construction. A second log building was moved on site, and the union of these structures now houses a gourmet kitchen and an indoor dining area, plus Anne's personal residence. The plank flooring, wood-burning stove, and period pieces give this "common" room a pioneer ambience—it's a place where guests watch culinary artistry in progress. The aromas of American country cooking fill the inn—apple-smoked pork loin, bean soup, bread pudding with whiskey sauce, or chicken with morel sauce.

The inn's garden supplies herbs, beans, peppers, eggplant, cucumbers, and tomatoes, and Anne prepares dishes with the local growing season in mind. She also invites guest chefs from Columbus and elsewhere to spend an evening in her kitchen, explaining their technique to guests as they perform their magic. Dinner is then served either in the common room, or out on a stone patio.

The Inn at Cedar Falls offers most unusual accommodations for its overnight guests. Housed in a modern, barn-shaped building are eight guest rooms (a ninth may be added). While similar in design to contemporary motel rooms, with individual heating and air conditioning units, they are furnished with antiques, and rough wood covers the floors. Each has an up-to-date private bath. Rocking chairs and tables make the second-floor balcony a delightful spot for reading or just soaking up the hilly landscape.

A section of the prairie meadow that predominates here has been mowed, so guests can stroll down the hill to an outstanding lookout. An adult-size swing hangs from a tree limb, next to an inviting hammock. In this spot, you might encounter deer, fox, or raccoon, while bird watchers view yellow finches, bluebirds, woodpeckers, ruffed grouse, and wild turkey.

Although the inn occupies a clearing right on Rte. 374, wooded hiking trails meander nearby. The Buckeye Trail, which connects Old Man's Cave with Ash Cave, is easily joined from here. Or hike to Rose Lake for some trout fishing. And cross-country skiing is a winter favorite.

Anne Castle wants her guests to enjoy the natural wonder of this area as much as she does. And while her kitchen primarily serves her overnight guests, others are welcome for dinner if they call ahead and make reservations. A single menu is prepared at mealtime, with one sitting when all Anne's visitors can come together to share their days' adventures. And special events including wine tastings (once a liquor license is secured), antique seminars, and arts and crafts displays at the inn are planned. Holidays are special times here—Anne wants to provide those without family nearby (or those escaping relatives!) a homey retreat full of holiday spirit.

The Inn at Cedar Falls is located at 21190 Rte. 374, 10 miles southwest of Logan; (614) 385-7489. Rates: $40–$45 single, $55–$60 double (includes breakfast). Visa and MasterCard are accepted. Open year-round.

Those seeking privacy and tranquility in the deep woods of the Hocking Hills will find them at **Bookman Woods**. Here four cabins lie nestled in the trees around a spring-fed lake. The cabins are well separated from one another, and each has a private dock on the lake—a perfect spot to fish for largemouth bass and bluegill or to launch one of the rowboats or canoes provided for guests. Lake swimming is a favorite summer pastime here, or you can loll and sunbathe out on the diving platform floating in the center of Bookman Lake. Whatever you choose to do here, the limited number of cabins insures that you will never encounter a crowd.

Gordon and Jennie Bookman acquired this property in the mid-1970s, when it had only one small cabin. Since then, Gordon has

expanded that original cabin and constructed three more, as well
as the Bookman residence. And when I say Gordon built these
structures, I'm not talking about someone who served as his own
contractor, overseeing carpenters, plumbers, and the like—he
personally erected each building, with virtually no assistance.
Gordon is a civil engineer who grew tired of the bureaucracy of
major road building projects and decided to create his own environment. And even though the Bookman property could easily
accommodate additional cabins or a camping area, Gordon and
Jennie have rejected that in order to insure that Bookman Woods
remains a quiet and peaceful escape from the rest of the world.

Cabins here range from one-bedroom single stories to the bi-
level Cedar House with two large decks, whirlpool, and two-plus
bedrooms. Each cabin at Bookman's has a deck, porch swing,
wood-burning stoves with glass fronts for fire watchers (as well
as electric heat), and outdoor barbecue grills. All are comfortably
furnished in pleasing earth tones, and they have plenty of windows looking out on the dense forest. Complete kitchens round
out the facilities here.

Bookman Woods is east of Laurelville, off of Rte. 180; (614)
332-9836 (telephone service in this area is notoriously
inconsistent—have the operator place this call for you if there's
no answer or you can't get through). Rates: $50–$100 per night,
depending on size of cabin, day of the week, and season. Master-
Card and Visa are accepted. Open year-round. Reservations are
required.

For years, Page and Vera Backus made plans for their 100
acres in the Hocking Hills, and those plans have come to fruition
at what they now call **Fallswood**. After building their own spacious hilltop A-frame home, they sprinkled the surrounding
woods with twenty A-frame chalets—three-room structures complete with lofts. Each chalet sleeps six, has a private deck, wood-
burning stove (plus central heating), and a fully equipped kitchen.

Fallswood's quiet, isolated location makes it an ideal year-
round getaway retreat. In addition to the Backus's property, 800
acres of state forest adjoin their land and are available for hiking
and exploration.

Fallswood is at 18905 Rte. 664, west of Logan; (614) 385-6517.
Rates: from $65 for two people for the first day to $270 for seven
days. Additional charge for each additional person. Special family
and winter rates are available. Reservations required.

The cabins at the **Echo Hills Ski Resort** are also near Hockings Hills State Park. Primarily used by skiers in winter, these cabins are available year-round. Each building has two units, with two double beds, kitchenette, and bathroom with shower.

The ski area offers four Alpine slopes, including the "expert" slope with a 280-foot drop over its 1,500-foot length. Echo Hills also has ski equipment rental and instruction and a cafeteria.

Echo Hills Ski Resort is at 9500 Bauer Road, Logan; (614) 385-8760. The cabins rent for $40 per night double occupancy (plus $10 per night for each additional person).

In addition to hiking and camping, canoeing and horseback riding are popular in the Hocking Hills. **Hocking Valley Canoe Livery** provides rental equipment along the picturesque Hocking River, with trips ranging from two hours to three days at rates from $13 to $40 per canoe. The Logan livery is at 31251 Chieftan Drive (614) 385-8685, 385-2503. Canoe rentals are available April through October.

The natural beauty of the Hocking Hills makes them an ideal place for trail riding, and horses are saddled up and ready to go at the stables of the **Hocking Valley Ranch**. The ranch is on Rte. 93, 8 miles south of Logan; (614) 385-8361, 385-7626. It is open weekends in May, September, and October and daily during the summer, 10 A.M.–5 P.M.

Fairfield County

The **Georgian**, an elegant two-story brick mansion, sits on a hill looking down on Lancaster's central business district, just as it has for the past 150 years. Constructed in 1833 for prominent businessman Samuel Maccracken, the Georgian mixes Federal architecture with Regency features and Empire furnishings. The Federal influence can be seen in the symmetrical placement of doors, windows, and fireplaces, while the Regency features are exemplified by the curved bay windows along the west wall. Classic Ionic columns, each containing a complete tree trunk for structural support, form the west portico.

Maccracken came to Lancaster from Big Springs, Pennsylvania, in 1810. Later elected to the state legislature, he introduced the bill funding construction of Ohio's canal system. While serving as Ohio Canal Funds Commissioner, Maccracken raised $6 million in Europe for the project.

The Georgian

Maccracken's thirteen-room mansion is furnished with handsome pieces dating from the mid-1800s, including some of Maccracken's possessions. The original pine floors and woodwork remain intact, as do the original doors, door frames, and ornate arches. The spiral staircase features a cherry spindle handrail, and a large skylight allows light to spill down the stairs.

Splendid blue marble fireplaces from the quarry in King of Prussia, Pennsylvania, grace the two large parlors, as do the matching French chandeliers (c. 1820). One of the upstairs bedrooms contains a fine Regency bed (c. 1800)—the type of bed preferred by generals in the Civil War, since it could be assembled and disassembled easily by the troops. One unique item in the museum is a 1792 senility cradle. Similar in design and function to a baby's cradle, these were used by old people who were no longer ambulatory.

Hanging on the wall in one of the stairways are original Fairfield County land grants signed by presidents Jefferson and Madison. Also on display is an American flag with eighteen stars—the flag of the United States from 1816 to 1820. The basement houses the kitchen, equipped as it was in the 1830s, and a unique dry well, where ground water from the surface drained by way of pipes and was dispersed into the ground beneath the basement.

The Georgian is at the corner of East Wheeling and North Broad streets, Lancaster; (614) 654-9923. Open March through December, Tuesday through Sunday, 1–4 P.M. (last tour at 3:15). Admission: adults, $1.50; children (under age sixteen), 75¢.

After your tour of the Georgian, be sure to walk up East Wheeling Street for a view of the magnificent restored homes in a hilly, shaded section of Lancaster. If lunch or dinner is the next item on your itinerary, try a 1940s hotel that is making a comeback. Just across the street from the Georgian, the **R.J. Pitcher Inn** features food, libations, and lodging in a delightful setting.

With rich wooden doors and trim, potted greenery, classy green and gold carpeting, and distinctive floral wall coverings, the main dining room of the hotel has candle-lit tables and indirect lighting, creating a cozy atmosphere. The dinner menu offers a variety of steaks, prime rib, seafood such as garlic broiled shrimp, and a half dozen fancy burgers. Pasta dishes, hot lobster salad, and grilled breast of duck with sauce moutard are also favorites.

Bartenders in the cheerful Hoddle Bar mix exotic concoctions including the powerful artillery punch—a potent blend of rum, brown sugar, tea, wine, orange juice, rye whiskey, and champagne. The less daring can sample the fish house punch—a more moderate mix of lemon, pineapple juice, rum, and peach brandy.

Both the Hoddle Bar and the dining room serve lunch, which features soups, salads, and sandwiches, plus entrees such as flank steak San Francisco, quiche, and fresh fish of the day.

The inn serves fresh homemade pies and cakes, and the walnut pie is a standout. Due to the popularity of lunch and dinner selections, the dining rooms accept reservations for both meals. The inn is popular with local people, so to avoid being turned away, make a reservation if possible.

The R.J. Pitcher Inn is at 123 North Broad Street, Lancaster; (614) 653-5522. Open for breakfast Monday through Friday, 7 A.M.–10:30 A.M.; for lunch Monday through Friday, 11 A.M.–2 P.M.; and for dinner Monday through Saturday, 5–10 P.M. Prices: lunch, inexpensive to moderate; dinner, moderate to expensive. Rooms at the inn range from $31 to $37 for those that have been restored and $21 to $26 for those awaiting restoration. MasterCard, Visa, and American Express are accepted.

Off the Beaten Path in Southwest Ohio

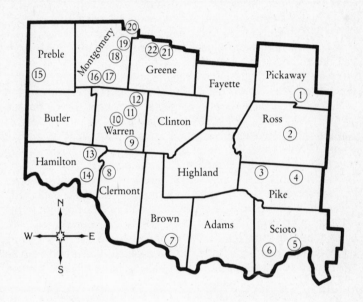

1. Circle K Ranch
2. Adena
3. Pike Lake State Park
4. Governor's Lodge/Lake White Club
5. Brewery Arcade
6. Shawnee State Park
7. Rankin House
8. Millcroft Inn/Piccadilli Tobacco Shop and Country Store
9. Valley Vineyards
10. Golden Lamb/Glendower
11. Stewart's Aviation
12. Waynesville
13. Montgomery Inn
14. Mariemont Inn and Lodge
15. Fairhaven
16. Florentine Hotel
17. Miamisburg Mound/Peerless Mill Inn
18. Carillon Historical Park
19. U.S. Air Force Museum
20. Carriage Hill Reserve
21. Clifton Gorge Nature Preserve/ Clifton Mill
22. Yellow Springs

Southwest Ohio

Pickaway County

Frazzled city folks can unwind and relax in a peaceful rural setting on Clifford and Marjorie Kerns's **Circle K Ranch**. On this working 200-acre farm, the Kerns family grows corn, wheat, soybeans, oats, and hay and tends cows, ducks, chickens, and goats, plus the eighteen horses and ponies available for trail riding.

The Kerns rent the 100-year-old, six-room tenant farm cottage just across the pond from their farmhouse. Modestly furnished, this two-story, white frame cottage has two bedrooms (with three double beds and a baby bed), a completely equipped kitchen, and all the necessary linens and blankets. Fans cool the cottage in summer, and the lack of heating restricts the season to the end of April through October.

Included in a weekly rental of the cottage is a daily morning trail ride through the meadows, woods, and creek beds on the Kerns's property (trail rides are $5 extra for those who rent the cottage for a weekend). Other activities at the Circle K include tennis on the farm's single court, volleyball, and swimming in the above-ground pool or in the farm pond. Stocked with bluegill, largemouth bass, and catfish, the pond also is a fine fishing hole. Every Sunday night, the Kerns host a cookout dinner and hayride for family and guests, and Clifford prepares homemade ice cream one night during the week.

The Kerns also offer supervised farm vacations for unaccompanied children, who spend a week living in the family farmhouse. For $200 to $225 per week, the kids receive all their meals and take advantage of the horseback riding, swimming, and fishing. All guests of Circle K are invited to participate in the daily farm chores and activities, including the planting and harvesting.

The cottage is available for full weeks only during the summer, and reservations should be made well in advance. The cottage can be rented for a full week or for a weekend in the spring and fall. Trail riding and riding lessons are offered to the public, by appointment only.

The Circle K Ranch is at 26525 Gay-Dreisbach Road, 5 miles south of Circleville; (614) 474-3711. The cottage rents for $225 per week for up to four people, $25 for each additional person; or for $20 per person for a Friday through Sunday weekend. Reservations are required.

Ross County

Thomas Worthington first came to Ohio from Virginia at the age of twenty-three in 1796, when he and a small band of men arrived to claim the land promised their fathers and friends after the Revolutionary War. Worthington permanently moved his family to Ohio in 1798 and quickly became active in the efforts to achieve statehood for the territory. He succeeded in that endeavor and served as a member of Ohio's Constitutional Convention in 1802. After being elected as one of the state's first United States senators, Worthington built his magnificent hilltop estate, **Adena**. Worthington and his wife, Eleanor, raised their ten children at Adena and entertained distinguished guests such as President James Monroe, Henry Clay, Aaron Burr, and the Indian chief Tecumseh. After building Adena, Worthingtron was reelected to the United States Senate in 1811, and later he served two terms as the governor of Ohio.

More than three-hundred of the estate's original 5,000 acres are now open to the public, and visitors explore the spacious, two-story sandstone home, the barn, the springhouse, and the smokehouse—all located in a rolling meadow above the Scioto River Valley. Self-guided tours of the eighteen-room home allow you to browse at your own pace, appreciating the fine antiques described on the fact sheet, which gives the style and origins of the furnishings in the home. While many of the pieces on display did not belong to the Worthingtons, they date from the 1780s to 1820s and are typical of the pieces used at Adena.

The large downstairs master bedroom, with its dark ash and oak floors, has a splendid view of the formal gardens. In an adjacent sitting room hangs a most unusual portrait of Thomas Jefferson, created not with paint, but with different colors of wool thread. The enormous state dining room features the actual dining table and chairs used at Adena in 1825. Two large portraits decorate the drawing room: one of Thomas Worthington at age twenty-five and the other of his sister, who married Edward Tiffin, Ohio's first governor.

Two of Adena's most interesting rooms are tucked away down the back stairs: the weaving room, with a large Virginia loom (c.

1790) and wool and flax wheels, and Worthington's private study. On display in the study is a tomahawk given to Worthington by Chief Tecumseh in 1807, and Worthington's musket and his father's sword still hang above the fireplace.

Across the meadow from the home is a scenic overlook of the Scioto River Valley—you can see for miles from this spot. In fact, the splendor of the sunrise over Mount Logan as viewed from Adena is said to have inspired the sunrise design incorporated in the seal of the state of Ohio.

Adena is off Rte. 104 on Allen Avenue, 3 miles north of Chillicothe; (614) 772-1500. Open from Memorial Day to Labor Day, Wednesday through Saturday, 9:30 A.M.–5 P.M.; Sunday, noon–5 P.M. May be open weekends in September and October. Admission: adults, $2; children (ages six to twelve), $1.

Shawnee War Chief Tecumseh dreamed of banding together 50,000 warriors from all the western Indian tribes in a force that he hoped would end the white man's westward expansion. The plan obviously failed, and the whites eventually conquered the land north and west of the Ohio River and beyond.

Tecumseh's story is portrayed nightly except Sundays during the summer at Sugarloaf Mountain Amphitheatre in the outdoor drama **Tecumseh!** On Sunday nights, the amphitheater presents the Tony Award-winning musical **Shenandoah**. The Tecumseh Restaurant Terrace serves a buffet dinner each evening prior to the 8 P.M. curtain.

Sugarloaf Mountain Amphitheatre is on Delano Road, east of Rte. 159, 6 miles northeast of Chillicothe; (614) 775-0700. Performances take place from early June to mid-September. Admission: adults, $8 to $9; children (ages ten and under), $6. Reservations recommended for weekend performances. Master-Card and Visa are accepted.

Pike County

When you're traveling through southern Ohio, you can't help but notice the dozens of lakes in the region—lakes providing boating, fishing, swimming, and other recreational activities. For this reason I heartily recommend that when you travel off the beaten path in southern Ohio, you always pack a swimsuit—particularly on hot summer days.

One of these alluring lakes is thirteen-acre Pike Lake in **Pike Lake State Park**, which offers a delightful spot for swimming, rowing, fishing, or scuba diving. Lifeguards watch over the sandy beach and swimming area during the summer, and rowboats can be rented. Anglers enjoy the catfish, largemouth bass, crappie, and bluegill, and divers take advantage of the remarkably clear water.

While the state park is a modest 600 acres, a densely wooded 10,600-acre state forest surrounds the park. There are numerous hiking trails in the state forest and 7 miles of trails in the park.

Up a shady hill from the lake sit the park's twenty-five rental cabins—twelve deluxe two-bedroom cabins and thirteen standard cabins. All are set in secluded locations, and the deluxe cabins offer completely equipped kitchens, baths, living areas, and screened porches. The standard cabins contain a single large sleeping and living area with four bunks and a fold-out couch, a kitchen, and bath. Pike Lake also has 150 campsites, and a park naturalist conducts nature programs during summer months.

Pike Lake State Park is at 1847 Pike Lake Road, 7 miles south of Bainbridge; (614) 493-2212. The standard cabins are available April through October; rates range from $36 per night to $156 per week. Rates for the deluxe cabins, which are open year-round, range from $48 per night to $198 per week. All cabins are rented for full weeks only during summer months. Early reservations recommended.

Bed and breakfast accommodations may be secured at nearby **Governor's Lodge** on Lake White. A weekend at Governor's Lodge is like spending time at a friend's spacious lake house. As you journey up the long driveway, you see what appears to be a large, two-story residence set on a wooded peninsula overlooking the lake. In fact, the lodge was originally built as a private residence in the 1930s, though it has been expanded and renovated several times over the years.

Since 1966, National Church Residences, a non-profit senior citizen housing organization, has operated the lodge, which offers a secluded and peaceful getaway. Each of the eight guest rooms has warm wood paneling and a spectacular view of the lake. The homey Lounge Room serves as a comfortable community living room, with unpretentious furnishings and a massive stone fireplace. The Lake Room is another gathering place for guests, and its wall of windows looks out on the tall hickories, buckeyes, and oaks that populate the peninsula. Between the lodge and the lake is a large "backyard" area, with picnic tables and lawn furniture—the perfect place for perusing the Sunday paper or enjoying a good book. A cottage, separated from the lodge, is popular with those celebrating anniversaries, honeymoons, and the like. A light breakfast of pastries, cereal, coffee, and juice is the only meal offered at the lodge, but many guests have dinner at the locally acclaimed Lake White Club, which is within easy walking distance of the lodge.

With its unlimited horsepower rating, the 350-acre Lake White is a popular waterskiing and speedboating reservoir during the summer. Governor's Lodge has a private boat dock, and a launching ramp is nearby.

Governor's Lodge is on Rte. 552, 2 miles south of Waverly; (614) 947-2266. Open year-round. Rates: $34 per night for one person plus $12 for each additional person (includes breakfast; no charge for children under eighteen). MasterCard and personal checks are accepted. Reservations recommended, particularly for weekend nights.

The **Lake White Club** dates back to 1935, but the building housing the club was a log cabin on Pee Pee Creek long before construction of the dam and spillway created Lake White. The lobby of the restaurant contains the original rough-hewn wooden beams of the cabin built on this spot in the 1820s. The Ohio and Erie Canal could be seen from the windows of that cabin; the canal followed the creek on its way south to Portsmouth. Pee Pee Creek received its name from the initials of Peter Patrick, which he carved in the trunk of a large beech tree beside the stream as a claim on this land in 1785, when this area was still Shawnee country.

The club specializes in down-home country cooking, and the chicken dinners (either fried or broiled) are a house specialty. Other entrees include half a dozen cuts of steak, chicken livers, hickory-smoked ham in raisin sauce, and ham and turkey smothered with a cheese sauce. If the 180-degree view of the lake whets your appetite for seafood, try the broiled or fried pickerel, the scallops, or the fried shrimp. The club offers prime rib as a special dinner every Saturday night.

The Lake White Club serves generous portions of all its entrees, and the light wood paneling and bentwood chairs give the dining room a pleasant, not-too-formal atmosphere.

The Lake White Club is on Rte. 552, 2 miles south of Waverly; (614) 947-5000. Open Tuesday through Saturday, 4–9 P.M.; Sunday, noon–8 P.M. Prices: moderate to expensive.

Scioto County

A former brewery in Portsmouth's Boneyfiddle Historical District now houses a fine selection of specialty shops. It's called the **Brewery Arcade**, and it's located in the old Portsmouth Brewing Company's brick building, which was constructed in 1842. Forty-seven years later, German Julius Esselborn purchased the plant, and he added the city's first ice-making facility in 1891, expanding the name of the firm to the Portsmouth Brewing and Ice Company. Esselborn and his son Paul successfully operated this business until Prohibition.

Over the years, a number of owners and businesses used the building, until the current proprietors purchased it in 1976. After extensive renovation, this historic structure now has a dozen unusual shops, a restaurant, and turn-of-the-century atmosphere. In this delightful indoor mall, with its rustic woods and brick floors, are gift shops, craft shops, and an antique shop. Cobblestone Leather offers hand-tooled belts, buckles, purses, and hats. Other shops include a Western shop loaded with hats, clothing, and Western accessories and P-town Imports, with its wide selection of turquoise and other fine jewelry.

The Brewery Arcade is one block from the Ohio River at 224 Second Street, Portsmouth; (614) 353-9121. Open Tuesday through Saturday, 10:30 A.M.–5:30 P.M.

Shawnee State Park, with more than 60,000 acres of parkland and adjoining state forest, consists of ridge upon ridge of thick woods in the splendid southern Ohio countryside. To get perspective on the size of this stunningly beautiful acreage, note that the park contains over 130 miles of roads, not to mention the miles of hiking and bridle paths. Shawnee is particularly popular in October, when the changing leaves produce hillsides bursting with reds, oranges, and golds. A 5,000-acre section of the park has been set aside as the Shawnee Wilderness Area, preserving the unspoiled natural beauty of the land. The park's two small lakes, Turkey Creek Lake and Roosevelt Lake, both have sandy swimming beaches.

A modern stone and timber fifty-room lodge provides overnight accommodations in this peaceful park, as do twenty-five deluxe two-bedroom cabins. Facilities at the lodge include an indoor and outdoor pool, tennis courts, a restaurant, a game room, and an eighteen-hole golf course with putting green, restaurant, and game room. Lodge rates are $52 per night, double occupancy. The cabins are tucked away in an isolated section of the park and come equipped with all kitchen utensils, linens, and blankets. Cabin rates range from $69 per night to $300 per week. Numerous campsites are also available.

Shawnee State Park is on Rte. 125, 12 miles west of Portsmouth; (614) 858-6621, 858-4561. Open year-round; reservations recommended.

Brown County

The red brick two-story house, with its shake roof and white trim, does not at first appear in any way extraordinary. It does offer a marvelous view down the steep hill to the Ohio River and across the river into northern Kentucky, but there is no outward evidence of this house's role in history. But 150 years ago, rickety wooden steps led from the river up the hillside to this modest home. Those steps became known as the "stairway to liberation," and on moonless nights slaves escaping from plantations in the South crossed the Ohio River and climbed those weathered steps to the **Rankin House,** home of Reverend John Rankin.

Rankin and his wife, Jean, were conductors on the Underground Railroad, which transported thousands of slaves to freedom in Canada. Rankin's battle against slavery began with his abolitionist preaching as early as 1815, and a series of his letters on the subject were published in a book in 1826. The home he built on "Liberty Hill" protected runaway slaves from the day it was completed in 1828 until 1863. Rankin used an elaborate set of signals with lanterns in his windows to communicate the "all clear" message to Alexander Campbell and other abolitionists in town.

Now open to the public as a museum, the Rankin House contains some of the Rankins' possessions, including John Rankin's personal bible, published in 1793. The house has dark hardwood floors and high ceilings typical of the period, as well as completely furnished bedrooms and a kitchen stocked with cooking utensils and equipment used in the mid-1800s.

One upstairs room houses a small abolitionist museum, which tells of the more than 2,000 slaves who stayed at Rankin House (often as many as twelve at a time) on their way to freedom. It was Reverend Rankin who told Harriet Beecher Stowe the account of a slave named Eliza who carried her children across the frozen, but thawing, Ohio River. Her bravery was rewarded—the bounty hunters pursuing her found the ice broken up by the time they reached the river next morning, forcing them to abandon their chase. Stowe immortalized the story of Eliza in her book *Uncle Tom's Cabin*. Because of his influence in the abolitionist movement and his work as a conductor on the Underground Railroad, Southern plantation owners offered a bounty for Rankin's life.

The Rankin House is just off Rte. 52, west of the central business district in Ripley; (513) 392-1627. Open Memorial Day to Labor Day, Wednesday through Sunday, noon–5 P.M. Admission: adults, $1; children, 50¢.

Clermont County

The historic structure that now houses the **Millcroft Inn** has been a centerpiece in Milford, Ohio, for generations. Construction was begun here in 1812, probably by Elijah and Cyrus Pierson, on what would at first be a commercial building. Wealthy John Kugler acquired the property in 1837, first using it as a general merchandise store, but later converting it into a palatial residence. The stables behind the Kugler mansion housed not only horses but also liquor—a distillery was one of Kugler's many business interests. The building served a variety of owners and purposes through the years (including a stint as a bordello) before it underwent a complete restoration in 1977.

Today owners Pamela and Stephen Gongola serve fine meals at this charming inn near the banks of the Little Miami River. Fresh flowers, candlelight, the rustic atmosphere of the tavern in the old stable—these elements create a peaceful harmony here. American cuisine is the order of the day, with an emphasis on freshness and meticulous preparation. You might want to lead off with an appetizer, perhaps the pasta du jour. Main course selections include steak Diane, fresh salmon or orange roughy, and intriguing veal dishes. Top off your meal with one of the tempting desserts—the blacktie cheesecake is a local favorite.

Piccadilli Tobacco Shop and Country Store

The Millcroft Inn is at 203 Mill Street, Milford; (513) 831-8654. Open for lunch, Monday through Saturday, 11 A.M.–3 P.M. Dinner is served Monday through Thursday, 5–10 P.M.; Friday and Saturday, 5–11 P.M.; Sunday, 4–9 P.M. Prices: lunch, inexpensive to moderate; dinner, expensive. MasterCard, Visa, and American Express are accepted. Reservations are recommended.

After dining at the Millcroft Inn, take time to walk through the historic Milford central business district. Housed in restored commercial buildings, stores on Main Street include Early Antiques, the AAA Saddle Shop with its complete selection of Western and leather goods, and a cheerful gift shop called 100 Main, which happens to be its address.

My favorite is around the corner at 207 Garfield: the **Piccadilli Tobacco Shop and Country Store**. The building dates back to the 1870s and has housed the Piccadilli since 1977. A complete tobacco and pipe shop occupies the front room; the remainder of the diverse inventory is in the two back rooms and in the basement, and there are four new shops on the second floor.

The shop contains baskets of all types, sizes, and shapes, including primitive-style ones. Other items include country tin, brass, and copper pieces, pottery, and hand-dipped beeswax candles. Splendid antiques abound here. Children are sure to enjoy the little wooden village of Cats Meow and meeting Lizzy and her wooden doll friends. Upstairs is a new Christmas shop, with plenty of gift and decorating ideas.

The Piccadilli Tobacco Shop and Country Store is at 207 Garfield, Milford; (513) 831-0181. Open Tuesday through Friday, 11 A.M.–5 P.M.; Saturday, 10 A.M.–4 P.M.

Warren County

On the last Thursday, Friday, and Saturday in September, **Valley Vineyards** hosts the annual Ohio Wine Festival, with live entertainment, judging of homemade wines, and other festivities. The rest of the year, Ken and Jim Schuchter's Valley Vineyards produces more than a dozen fine wines from its forty-five acres of American and French hybrid grapes.

Grape growing and wine making have been popular in southern Ohio for more than a hundred and fifty years, and the Schuchters planted their first vines at Valley Vineyards in 1969. The winery, in a restored barn, offers a tasting tray with one-ounce servings of twelve different wines—the perfect way to investigate and appreciate the vineyard's quality blends. I particularly enjoyed the Ohio Sauterne—a full-bodied, medium dry white wine from the French hybrid Villard Blanc grape.

The winery has indoor and outdoor seating, with occasional cookout dinners on the large patios. Cheese plates and pizzas are always available.

Valley Vineyards is on Rtes. 22 and 3, Morrow; (513) 899-2485. Open Monday through Thursday, 11 A.M.–8 P.M.; Friday and Saturday, 11 A.M.–11 P.M.

On Dec. 23, 1803, Jonas Seaman received a license to operate a "house of public entertainment" at the site today occupied by one of Ohio's premier historic hotels, the **Golden Lamb**. The present building replaced Seaman's cabin in 1815, and the Lamb now provides travelers with fine dining and period accommodations in picturesque Lebanon, Ohio.

During its 175 years, distinguished guests at the Golden Lamb have included ten American presidents, Henry Clay, Mark Twain (who performed at the Lebanon Opera House in the late nineteenth century), and Charles Dickens, who, it is told, complained vociferously during his visit in 1842 when informed that the inn did not serve "spirits." Dickens would maintain his composure if he visited the Golden Lamb today, for the Black Horse Tavern provides complete bar service at the inn. And after some "refreshment," he might well enjoy browsing in the extensive gift shop on the lower level.

With a reputation for preparing challenging dishes, the Lamb offers a dinner menu that includes delights such as timbale of filet of sole and salmon mousse with lobster sauce; roast duckling; broiled veal medallion topped with asparagus, crabmeat, and bearnaise sauce; and roast leg of spring lamb with mint jelly. More traditional entrees include steaks, ham, roast pork loin with dressing, and baked filet of haddock. Lunch is also served at the Golden Lamb, with tasty soups, salads, and sandwiches, plus luncheon entrees including broiled petite filet mignon with bearnaise sauce and roast chicken with dressing.

After your meal in one of the four cozy downstairs dining areas, venture past the classy blue-gray lobby and up the stairs to the second floor. There you will discover five opulent private dining rooms. One is the Henry Clay Room (he visited the inn frequently on his trips between Kentucky and Washington, D.C.).

Decorated in cool greens and yellows, this room is furnished with a gorgeous dark hardwood table and matching chairs for ten. With their splendid period pieces, these private dining rooms truly conjure up images of a bygone era.

The second floor also has the most expensive guest room at the inn—the Charles Dickens Room. The massive carved headboard towers 12 feet in the air, as do the mirror and frame on the marble-topped washstand. The third and fourth floors contain the other seventeen guest rooms, each unique in its appointments and named for one of the noteworthy guests who have stayed at the Golden Lamb. The Dewitt Clinton Room, for example, is named for the New York governor who traveled to Lebanon in 1825 to attend the opening of the Ohio canal system and is furnished with a canopied four-poster bed and antique oak chests.

The fourth floor of the Lamb also houses the inn's Shaker museum, which is full of pieces collected from the former Shaker community called Union Village. The Shakers migrated to Warren County from New Lebanon, New York, and established a religious communal village. But one of their religious convictions was celibacy, which doomed the sect to a relatively short existence.

Shaker furnishings are simple and functional, devoid of ornamentation. The Shaker Pantry has the characteristic wall pegs for hanging utensils, herbs, and even chairs not in use. The Shaker Retiring Room contains a simple rope spring bed with trundle, a maple rocker, a pine cupboard, and a very rare maple and pine Shaker sewing desk. Perhaps the most interesting display room—Sarah's Room—belonged to Sarah Stubbs, a young girl who came to live in the hotel with her aunt and uncle after the death of her father in 1883. The room has the furniture which was Sarah's 100 years ago.

The Golden Lamb is at 27 South Broadway, Lebanon; (513) 932-5065. Prices: lunch, inexpensive to moderate; dinner, moderate to expensive. Lodging rates: $50 to $58 per night. MasterCard, Visa and American Express are accepted.

On a bluff overlooking Lebanon just a few blocks south of the Golden Lamb sits one of the best examples of Greek revival architecture in the Midwest: **Glendower**. Constructed by John Milton Williams, a young attorney, for approximately $5000 in 1836, the residence was inhabited by the Williams family during John Williams's career as county prosecutor and state legislator. Brigadier

Gen. Durbin Ward, another influential area politician, purchased Glendower from Williams, and the home remained in the Ward family until the turn of the century.

Knowledgeable guides lead visitors through the 14 rooms and basement, explaining the history and significance of the lavish furnishings, most of which date from the mid-1800s. In the downstairs drawing rooms, the symmetry characteristic of Greek revival architecture is readily apparent, with matching placement of doors, mirrors and fireplaces; one side of these rooms is the mirror image of the other. The original brass deadbolt still secures the front door, and the luxurious ash and walnut floors were installed when the home was built. The formal dining room contains a silver sugar bowl with a lock on it (to keep the servants from pilfering this then-expensive commodity), and the old Regina music box plays flat metal discs as it has for decades.

In addition to the furnished bedrooms upstairs, one room has a sizable collection of antique dolls and the 1865 sewing machine that won first prize at the Warren County fair. The basement display cases contain pioneer tools such as axes, woodworking equipment and a carpenter's vise. Other items include old-fashioned irons, candle molds, boot jacks, spectacles and snuff boxes, plus the compass used to plat the village of Lebanon and a wonderful assortment of fancy hand-turned horseshoes made by Matt Burdett, the village smithy in the 1890s.

Glendower is on Orchard Avenue off Rte. 48, just south of the business district in Lebanon; (513) 932-5366. Open from June through October, Tuesday through Saturday, 10:00 A.M.–4 P.M.; Admission: adults, $2.; children (ages 6 to 12),$1.

Would you like someone to take $105 from you and then push you out of an airplane flying at 3200 feet? That's precisely what they will do at the **Waynesville Sport Parachute Club** at the Waynesville airport. The club offers classes in skydiving every weekend morning at 11 a.m. (weekdays by appointment), and after four or five hours of expert instruction, you're ready to make your first jump! Though the club remained open all winter in past years, they may be closed during the coldest winter months.

If you would rather fly in a plane than jump from one, rent a glider (and instructor, if needed) from **Stewart's Aviation Service**, also at the Waynesville airport. Capture the thrill of soaring for as little as $25 (includes instructor). Unlike many soaring groups around the state, Stewart's is not a club (so there are no membership dues), but, rather, is an aircraft rental business.

Stewart's Aviation Service is at the Waynesville Airport on Rte. 42, south of Waynesville; (513) 897-7717 (gliders), (513) 897-3851 (skydiving). Stewart's is open daily from 10 A.M. until dark. Master-Card and Visa are accepted (for both glider rentals and skydiving).

With more antique shops per square mile than any other city or town in Ohio, Waynesville is a browser's paradise. Waynesville has over 30 individual shops, plus three large buildings where dozens of other dealers display their goods on consignment, and has become a major antique marketplace, attracting out-of-state buyers and Ohioans alike. Waynesville's antique boom started inauspiciously in the mid-1960s with the opening of a handful of shops, but the number has grown steadily ever since. Now, many of the town's commercial buildings, a substantial number of former residences and even one of the town's churches house antique stores—in fact, in one block on Main Street, there are nine shops in a row!

Among the many quality shops, two of my favorites sit next door to one another at 274 and 296 S. Main Street—**Spencer's Antiques** and **Vi's Antiques**. Vi, one of the original dealers in town, specializes in colored "depression glassware," and her shop contains an extensive collection of the red, amber, blue, and green plates, cups and saucers made in the late '20s and early '30s. She also stocks old bottles, tins, jars and many antique dolls and clocks. Vi's is open Monday through Saturday, 10 A.M.–5 P.M.

Next door, the two-story house with the large front porch holds the impressive inventory of Spencer's Antiques (actually, some of the inventory spills out into the front yard). Careful perusal of the ground floor, second floor and basement of this shop, with its hundreds of items, takes time, but it will be time enjoyably spent. George and Fay Spencer's inventory includes a large selection of oak—tables, chairs, washstands, chests, wardrobes and beds—plus many large walnut and poplar pieces. The basement is filled with old trunks, toys and stained glass, while the second floor has many antique kitchen gadgets such as meat and sausage grinders, iron pots and skillets. Spencer's acquires most of its inventory from southwestern Ohio, and this merchandise can be seen from noon to 5 P.M. daily. Be sure to check out the Spencer's other Waynesville antique shops—Spencer's Too (273 S. Main) and Spencer's Heirlooms (92 N. Main).

Many visitors to Warren County are attracted to the area because of southern Ohio's most popular amusement park complex—**Kings Island**. Its six themed areas, dozens of rides including five coasters (the Beast has been rated by the *Guiness Book of World Records* as the highest, longest and fastest roller coaster on earth), live shows, international shops and restaurants delight the thousands who visit the park during its May through September season. Kings Island is on I-71 at Kings Mills; (513) 241-5600.

Hamilton County

If you're in the mood for mouth-watering barbecued ribs and chicken, plus ice cold beer, try Ted Gregory's **Montgomery Inn**. This popular restaurant claims to serve the "world's greatest ribs," a designation with which few customers would argue. While the menu at the Montgomery Inn does include selections such as steaks, pork chops and filet of sole, the restaurant is known for the tender ribs and chicken dripping with a zesty sauce.

While waiting in the bar for your table, you'll see photographs of the likes of Tommy Lasorda and Billy Carter displayed on the wall, each autographed and extolling the virtues of Ted Gregory's barbecue. On the rough wood paneling in the comfortable dining rooms are photos and paintings of Gregory's other passion— horse racing. You'll even find some bridles and jockeys' jackets displayed throughout the inn.

For those unable to decide between barbecued ribs and barbecued chicken, try some of each with the half and half dinner, which is served with a crisp tossed salad and their famous Saratoga chip potatoes. The management thoughtfully provides bibs for those partaking of the sauce-laden barbecue.

For those not hungry for barbecue (which seems inconceivable once you experience the aroma in this restaurant), other menu selections include Cantonese-style fried oriental shrimp with sweet 'n' not sauce, Wisconsin's pride duckling and a number of sandwiches (including a barbecued beef sandwich).

The Montgomery Inn is at 9440 Montgomery Road (exit 12, east of Interstate 71), Montgomery; (513) 791-3482. Open Monday through Thursday, 11 A.M.–11 P.M.; Friday, 11 A.M.–midnight Saturday, 4 P.M.–midnight and Sunday, 4:00–9:30 P.M. Closed on Sunday during summer months. Prices: inexpensive to moderate. MasterCard and Visa are accepted.

The founders of the Mariemont Company designed and constructed the village of Mariemont as a totally planned community

Mariemont Inn and Lodge

modeled after the "garden city" villages in England. In the 1920s, they envisioned Mariemont as a rural alternative to bustling Cincinnati nearby.

While it's no longer in the country (Mariemont is now in the suburban ring surrounding Cincinnati), this quaint village, with its English Tudor commercial buildings and peaceful, tree-lined residential neighborhoods, does provide the tranquil existence sought by its founders. The entire village is listed on the National Register of Historic Places.

The **Mariemont Inn** offers visitors a charming place to imbibe, dine and spend the night. It is set facing the circle in the center of the commerical business district, and the striking Tudor exterior is rivaled by the interior decor in this classic structure. Each of the 60 guest rooms contains the dark, heavy woods and rich colors typical of the Tudor period; the spacious suites come furnished with ornate canopy beds, and there are antiques throughout the inn. Your day starts off with complimentary coffee or juice, delivered to your room at your convenience.

Visitors unwind in the cozy old-English pub, and the popularity of the dining room for breakfast, lunch, and dinner with area residents and business people speaks for the excellent food. An innovative breakfast-brunch-lunch menu featuring omelets, fritats, homemade soups, fine salads and a wide selection of sandwiches is served from 6:30 A.M. until 2 P.M. The varied dinner selections include fresh seafood, pasta, veal and many great steaks, with appetizers and desserts to accompany these dishes.

After your meal, enjoy a stroll, jog or bike ride in this picturesque village, or stop by the gift shop, bookstore, ice cream parlor, or other shops adjacent to the inn. Though downtown Cincinnati is only 15 minutes from the inn, when your walking through this peaceful community, the big city seems worlds away.

The Mariemont Inn is at 6880 Wooster Pike (Rte. 50), Mariemont; (513) 271-2100 (or call Best Western Reservations, (800) 528-1234). Breakfast, lunch and dinner prices are moderate to expensive. Lodging rates: $39 to $65 per night. MasterCard, Visa and American Express accepted.

Preble County

Every Sunday, the quiet, rural community of **Fairhaven** becomes a prime antique-lover's stop; a dozen shops are scattered throughout town. Several of these are in the former schoolhouse, including my favorite, **First Grade Antiques**. In this town two miles from the Indiana border, Ed and Bea Schoeneweiss's First Grade Antiques contains a vast quantity of oak pieces at very reasonable prices. The Schoeneweisses acquire most of their inventory, which includes dozens of ice boxes, tables, chairs and chests, from within a 100-mile radius, and they sell 85 percent of their goods to out-of-state dealers (an indication of their relatively low prices).

First Grade Antiques is on Rte. 177, Fairhaven; (513) 233-0869 (home phone). Open Saturday and Sunday, 10:30 A.M.–4 P.M. (All of Fairhaven's antique dealers are open on Sundays, some on Saturdays as well.)

Another intriguing shop is John Auraden's **Bunker Hill House**, built as a tavern in 1832. John has stocked his eight-room shop with all types of country furnishings and accessories,

including a large selection of "in the rough" pieces. Not everything is rough, however—during my last visit the Bunker Hill
House contained a magnificent $12,000 billiard table dating from
the 1890s and a $7200 three-mirror back bar from an old barber
shop.

The Bunker Hill House is on Rte. 177, Fairhaven; (513) 796-
3921. Open every Sunday afternoon or by appointment.

Montgomery County

Germantown's **Florentine Hotel** has been a part of that community almost since the town's inception. Philip Gunkel and a
group of settlers arrived from Pennsylvania in 1804, and Gunkel
apparently built the original brick section of the hotel in 1816.
William Leighty puchased the hotel in 1862 and modestly renamed it the Leighty House, a name it retained until the turn of
the century.

The first 70 years of the twentieth century were not as kind to
the Florentine. With nearly 40 different owners over the years, the
hotel declined and finally closed in 1974. After three full years of
renovation and restoration, the Florentine Hotel, now part of a
20-building National Historic District, reopened as a full sevice
restaurant in 1979.

The hotel serves meals and spirits either in the Tavern, with its
impressive bar, rough beams and hardwood floors, or in the dining rooms. The Tavern's exposed brick walls and large fireplace
create a casual atmosphere, while the dining rooms' period wallpapers provide a more formal setting.

The lunch menu consists of salads, a dozen different sandwiches and entrees such as broiled pork chops, baked scrod, and
chicken dishes. Dinner selections include baked stuffed sole and
shrimp, garlic saute of shrimp, scallops, chicken and chops. The
hotel offers four cuts of steak and serves homemade chocolate
mousse, ice cream and other dessert specialties.

The Florentine Hotel is at 21 West Market Street, Germantown;
(513) 855-7225. Open Tuesday through Thursday, 11:30 A.M.–9
P.M.; Friday and Saturday, 4:30–10:30 P.M.; Sunday 10 A.M.–7 P.M.
Prices: lunch, inexpensive; dinner, moderate to expensive. Master-
Card and Visa are accepted. Reservations recommended.

The community just east of Germantown has the largest coni-
cal burial mound in Ohio—the **Miamisburg Mound.** Artifacts

excavated from this 68-foot-high mound, which contains 54,000 cubic yards of earth, indicate the Adena Indians built it sometime between 1000 B.C. and A.D. 100. With a circumference of nearly 900 feet at the base, the mound had two burial vaults in it: one eight feet from the top of the mound which contained a bark-covered skeleton, the other 36 feet down and surrounded by logs but without any skeletal remains.

Visitors to the mound, which today is overgrown with brush and trees, can climb 116 steps to the top of this impressive earth-work for a splendid view of the Miami Valley. A 36-acre park encircles the mound, with picnic tables, barbecue grills and shelter houses.

The Miamisburg Mound is one mile south of Rte. 725 on E. Mound Avenue, Miamisburg. Open daylight hours, no admission charge.

After climbing the mound, you may want to stop for lunch or dinner at Miamisburg's **Peerless Mill Inn**. A huge waterwheel and the flowing Miami and Erie Canal once powered this former lumber mill (built in 1828). The building was converted into a restaurant 100 years later, the called the Peerless Pantry.

Inside this historic structure, the dining rooms have the original heavy beams, flagstone floors and four great stone fireplaces. Enhancing the nineteenth-century charm of the place, dried flowers hang form the walls, old wagon wheels form the lighting fixtures, and a flintlock musket is mounted over one of the fire-places. Fresh flowers trim each table in the five dining areas and in the dark, but friendly, tavern.

Country favorites including roast turkey and celery dressing and steaks dominate the menu, along with classy seafood and sophisticated dishes such as veal gruyere—veal topped with cheese, tomato and a light brown sauce. The house specialty is roast duckling, served with wild rice, orange sauce and corn fritters. Diners receive a delicious house seven-layer salad with their meal. The inn serves generous portions of its entrees.

Be sure to try the homemade chowder before your dinner and the daily fresh cobbler for dessert. Luncheon selections include burgers, sandwiches and salads (such as the turkey pecan salad), plus entrees including omelets and shrimp and sea scallop kabob.

The Peerless Mill Inn is at 319 South Second Street, Miamisburg; (513) 866-5968. Open for lunch Tuesday through Friday, 11 A.M.–2 P.M.; brunch, Sunday, 11 A.M.–2 P.M.; and dinner, Tuesday through Thursday, 5–9 P.M.; Friday and Saturday, 5–10 P.M.; Sunday, 1–7 P.M. Prices: lunch, inexpensive to moderate; dinner, moderate to expensive. MasterCard, Visa and American Express are accepted.

Across the Great Miami River from downtown Dayton in a rolling meadow, a 151-foot-high, 40 bell carillon stands as the landmark entrance to Carillon Historical Park. The Carillon was built by Colonel Edward Deeds and his wife. Free concerts delight audiences here from May through October.

In addition to the bells, this 65-acre park has an outstanding group of exhibit buildings, primarily dedicated to Dayton's contributions to the field of transportation. The museum's crown jewel has to be the Wright brother's Flyer III airplane in Wright Hall, which is nestled in the park's shady hillside. Weighing 900 pounds and incorporating for the first time aileron and rudder control systems, this plane was the world's first practical aircraft and is the one that Orville described as the plane on which he and Wilbur learned to fly. Two years after their historic 1903 flight at Kitty Hawk, Orville stayed aloft in the Flyer III for 38 minutes at an average speed of 40 miles per hour. Orville Wright later supervised the original restoration of this aircraft.

Deed's Barn, named for the park's primary benefactors, displays items from the two corporations profoundly influenced by Colonel Deeds and his contemporary Charles F. Kettering, the noted scientist and humanitarian. Both were employed by the National Cash Register Company of Dayton, and NCR gave Kettering the task of electrifying the cash register. Deed's Barn displays the result of that labor—the 1905 model first electrified.

Kettering and Deeds went on to found Dayton Engineering Lab (later called Delco), which revolutionized automobile ignition, starting and lighting systems. Deed's Barn contains a 1912 Cadillac—the first production auto to have these innovations.

The two-story log building called Newcom Tavern housed Dayton's first courthouse and tavern in 1796. The tavern includes many of its original items, such as the pewter ware used by Colonel and Mrs. Newcom, the colonel's favorite rocking chair and a 1798 wedding vest which belonged to the carpenter who built the tavern.

Other displays in Carillon Park include locomotives and railroad cars, a restored canal lock and covered bridge, a working gristmill, a blacksmith shop and a replica of the Wright brothers' bicycle shop. The Dayton Sales Company automobile showroom has a 1910 Speedwell, a 1923 Maxwell and a very rare 1908 Stoddard-Dayton (which sold for $2700 in its day).

Carillon Historical Park is at the intersection of Patterson and Carillon boulevards east of I-75 at the Edwin Moses/Nicholas Road exit, Dayton; (513) 293-3412. The park is open May 1 to Oct. 31, Tuesday through Saturday, 10 A.M.–6 P.M.; Sunday, 1–6 P.M. No admission charge.

For a look at more modern modes of transportation, be sure to see the 200 missiles and aircraft displayed at the impressive **U.S. Air Force Museum**. With 300,000 square feet of exhibit space in the two main hangar-type bays, plus the annex hangars, this has to be the world's most complete aviation museum. From a Wright Brother's original to an Apollo space capsule, the museum contains an incredibly comprehensive collection of flying machines. Spads, Camels, Spitfires, Mustangs, the B-29 that dropped the atomic bomb on Nagasaki in 1945 and the enormous Strategic Air Command B-36 bomber—all of these are in one museum.

Located only three miles from the place where the Wright Brothers tested their early designs, the museum, in addition to the aircraft, balloons and missiles, has dozens of exhibits that chronicle the history and milestones of aviation.

The U.S. Air Force Museum is at Wright-Patterson Air Force Base, off Rte. 4 east of Dayton; (513) 255-3284. Open daily except Christmas, weekdays, 9 A.M.–5 P.M.; weekends, 10 A.M.–6 P.M. No admission charge.

Daniel Arnold established his 158-acre family farm in 1830 and constructed a farmhouse six years later. The Arnold family worked the farm until 1910, and today this entire farmstead is being restored to its appearance in the 1880s. It's called **Carriage Hill**, and it's part of an 800-acre reserve.

The farmhouse contains pioneer equipment typical of the nineteenth century—quilting frame, wood-burning stove, and a firebox—while bubbles and imperfections in the house's window glass identify it as original. During hot weather, the Arnolds prepared their meals at the outdoor "summer kitchen" to avoid further heating the farmhouse; on many weekends, volunteers at the reserve now use that oven to bake fresh bread.

Other demonstrations at Carriage Hill include a blacksmith who operates the old bellows and a woodworker who shapes furniture on a foot-powered lathe. Like any 1880s farm, Carriage

Hill has a variety of farm animals: cattle, chickens, horses, sheep, and pigs. The horses are used to give hayrides through the reserve's lush meadows and woods. Hiking and bridle trails also wind through the reserve's acreage. Special events such as square dances, cider pressing, and old-fashioned wheat threshing take place throughout the year at Carriage Hill.

Carriage Hill Reserve is at 7860 Shull Road, north of I-70 off Rte. 201, Dayton; (513) 879-0461. The reserve is open daily except Christmas and New Year's Day, 8 A.M.–dusk. Farmhouse tours are available daily, 10 A.M.–5 P.M.; hayrides and craft demonstrations take place on weekends, 1–5 P.M. No admission charge.

Greene County

You have to give **Clifton Mill** credit—it has burned down twice, but it has always come back. The first water-powered gristmill at this site on the Little Miami River was built in 1803. Called Davis Mill for its founder Owen Davis, this first mill prospered until destroyed by fire in the 1840s. But a year or two later, a second mill was erected here, a mill that did its part for the Union Army by providing cornmeal and flour to Federal troops during the Civil War.

However, this mill burned down about the time the Confederacy was defeated. In 1869, the Armstrong family built a third mill on this site, which they sold to Issac Preston twenty years later.

Three generations of Prestons operated the mill until 1948. And although it avoided catching fire again, Clifton Mill did sit idle, deteriorating for fifteen years, until Robert Heller bought it and breathed life into it once again.

Today visitors enjoy self-guided tours of this impressive six-story power plant. The mill generates all its own electricity, and the huge James Leffel Company turbine on the lowest level, installed in 1908, once provided electricity for farms, homes, and businesses in Clifton, Cedarville, and Yellow Springs at a very modest $1 per month per customer.

Clifton Mill grinds flour, cornmeal, and pancake mix as it has for decades, a process you observe during your tour. And meal and flour, along with homemade breads, pies, and other pastries, are available for purchase, as are fine jams, jellies, syrups, teas, spices, and other specialties. Clifton Mill also has a short-order kitchen, which serves breakfast, soups, sandwiches, and salads, plus ice cream. On a nice day, take your meal or snack out on the Millrace Deck, and listen to water rushing under your feet on its way to the turbines. The former owner's residence has recently been converted into a cozy pub with wood floors and a fabulous fireplace.

Clifton Mill is located at 75 Water Street (Rte. 72), Clifton; (513) 767-5501. Mill tours: adults, 75¢; children, 50¢. Open seven days a week, 9 A.M.–6 P.M., (9 A.M.–8 P.M. summer months).

Designated as a Natural Landmark by the National Park Service, the **Clifton Gorge Nature Preserve** rates as some of Ohio's most beautiful public land. Over the years, the swift Little Miami River has carved a deep gorge through the thick forest, a process started by the raging meltwaters of the last retreating glacier. The power of the river once turned the wheels of two gristmills in the area—Clifton Mill, which has been restored in the nearby village of Clifton, and a second mill, the remains of which are still visible in the gorge.

With the clean, vertical drops of the limestone cliffs, Clifton Gorge ranked high with rock climbers until that activity was banned in 1982. Concern for the nearly 350 different wildflowers in the park, which provide an unparalleled spring wildflower display, prompted the rock-climbing prohibition.

The preserve has miles of hiking trails along both rims of the gorge and following the river at the floor of the canyon. The adjacent John Bryan State Park contains twelve additional hiking trails, campsites, and picnic areas.

Clifton Gorge Nature Preserve is on Rte. 343, just west of Clifton. The entrance to John Bryan State Park is on Rte. 370, near Clifton; (513) 767-1274. Open daylight hours, no admission charge.

Known as a hotbed of anti-war and counter-culture activity in the sixties and early seventies, Yellow Springs remains slightly eccentric. The marchers and demonstrators have been replaced by potters and shopkeepers, but Antioch College still provides the youthful emphasis of this uncommon community.

The town has a pleasant shopping area called the **Kings Yard**, which is a cluster of stores connected by brick walkways under tall shade trees. Bonadies Glasstudio stocks original stained-glass lamps, windows, and boxes, while Yellow Springs Pottery has handcrafted vases and plant and candle holders. Delicate herbs, spices, teas, and sachets can be bought at No Common Scents.

The Yard's two bookstores sell both new and used titles. Mysteries from the Yard specializes in all manner of suspense and mystery works, and the Epic Bookstore carries a diverse inventory including feminist and occult books.

The true jewel of the Yard is a quiet restaurant set in the trees away from the street—the **Winds Cafe**. The thicket of greenery surrounding the cafe isolates it from the noises of the outside world, providing a tranquil setting for fine cooking.

Stained glass, ceiling fans, hardwood floors, and fresh flowers on the candle-lit tables set the casual tone of the cafe, which has been operating since 1977. The eclectic mix of dining tables and chairs, some with tablecloths, some without, complete the relaxed atmosphere.

From the appetizers such as baked brie (served with fresh fruit and French bread) to the house specialty dessert, chocolate mousse, the kitchen carefully prepares the frequently changing menu. On my visit, the evening entrees were chicken Kiev, salad nicoise and, my selection, coquille Saint Jacques. A light and delicately seasoned wine sauce embellished this dish of scallops, served in a large pottery half-shell. In summer, try the fresh cold soups such as strawberry-melon—they are exquisite!

The classy bar serves exotic concoctions, such as golden dream (a thick combination of galliano, triple sec, orange juice, and cream) and south wind (a frothy blend of rum, tequila, cointreau, and orange juice). Luncheon offerings include soups, salads, omelets, and daily specials. Innovative sandwiches range from curry chicken salad to the organic sandwich: cheese, tomato, cucumber, sprouts, onions, and sunflower seeds.

The Winds Cafe is at 230 Xenia Avenue, Yellow Springs; (513) 767-1144. Lunch served Monday through Saturday, noon–2 P.M.; dinner, Monday through Saturday, 6–10 P.M.; Sunday brunch, 10 A.M.–1:30 P.M. Prices: lunch, inexpensive; dinner, moderate. MasterCard and Visa are accepted.

A second Yellow Springs eatery of note, even more casual than the Winds Cafe, is just a couple of blocks away: **Carol's Kitchen**. Here you serve yourself from a spectacular spread of homemade salads and sandwich fixings, but one word of caution: You are charged by the ounce—this isn't an unlimited salad bar as in some fast food places. And your selections aren't like fast food either—carefully prepared and seasoned salads of every description (including fine crab and shrimp salads), fresh fruits, and innovative soups such as vegetarian cheddar potato (delightful).

Carol's is also a complete bakery, so your sandwich starts with slices of just-from-the-oven onion dill, honey wheat, pumpernickel, country rye, or six-grains bread, also sold by the loaf. Top off your meal with a Soho Soda or Perrier.

Once you've made your selections, it's off to the enclosed patio to enjoy them. This fabric-topped area lets in plenty of light while keeping the rain away. And that light is necessary for the plants that fill every available space. There are hanging plants, potted plants, plants on the tables—plants that create a lush, almost tropical, ambiance.

Carol's Kitchen is on Corry Street at Dayton Street, Yellow Springs; (513) 767-1030. Open Monday through Friday, 11 A.M.–8 P.M.; Saturday, 10 A.M.–8 P.M.

If you've decided you need more time to explore the Yellow Springs area, spend the night at the historic **Morgan House**. No Ohio town seems more suited to the bed-and-breakfast concept than this one, and Morgan House fits the bill perfectly. Built in 1921 for the president of Antioch College, Arthur Morgan, this substantial two-story structure has a huge screened porch, a perfect spot to enjoy a morning cup of coffee or the evening breeze.

Innkeeper Marianne Britton has created an appropriately peaceful setting with cozy furnishings, including Ohio antiques. Located on a quiet residential street just blocks from the business district, Morgan House features four guest rooms.

Morgan House is at 120 West Limestone Street, Yellow Springs; (513) 767-7509. Rates: single, $35; double, $40; includes continental breakfast.

Off the Beaten Path
in West Central Ohio

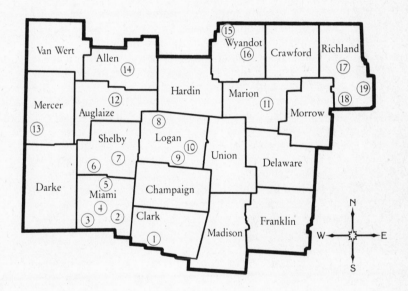

1. Young's Jersey Dairy Farm Store
2. West Milton Inn
3. Brukner Nature Center
4. Stillwater Wineries
5. Piqua Historical Area
6. Vinterra Farm Winery and
   Vineyard
7. Sidney Dairy
8. O'Connor's Landing/Wicker
   Resort
9. Zane Caverns
10. Piatt Castles
11. Harding Home and Memorial/
    Stengle-True Museum
12. Neil Armstrong Air and Space
    Museum
13. Fort Recovery State Museum
14. Allen County Museum
15. Indian Trail Caverns
16. Indian Mill State Memorial
17. Frederick Fitting House
18. Malabar Farm and Inn
19. Kingwood Center

West Central Ohio

Clark County

Just up the road from Yellow Spring's Antioch College (and across the Greene County–Clark County line) is a most remarkable twenty-four–hour store—**Young's Jersey Dairy Farm Store**. Located at a working dairy, Young's caters to the nearby college crowd and the area's year-round residents with fresh breads and pastries, fountain service, and dairy-fresh milk and cream—all available at any hour of the day or night!

Young's bakes from scratch the vast selection of doughnuts and pastries—turnovers, brownies, pies, creme horns, pecan rolls, coffee cake, fudge, and cookies, plus glazed, whole wheat, powdered, jelly-filled, and cinnamon doughnuts. The fountain offers shakes, splits, sundaes, and ice cream sodas. The shakes are particularly good—made in every flavor imaginable using farm-fresh milk. Served regular or extra thick, the calf shake has two scoops of ice cream, the cow shake comes loaded with four scoops, and the diet-busting bull shake contains five scoops.

The selection of fresh breads includes white, garlic, rye, french, nut, whole wheat, raisin, and cinnamon, as well as hamburger buns and dinner rolls. Young's also sells an assortment of homemade pasta. Seating is provided both indoors and at picnic tables not far from the dairy barn.

Young's Jersey Dairy Farm Store is on Rte. 68 just north of the Greene County–Clark County line, in Hustead; (513) 325-0629.

Miami County

Abundant quantities of outstanding country cooking in a scenic setting—that's what you can expect from the Mote family's **West Milton Inn**. Established in 1927 (in a building that's even older), the inn has no formal menu. Your waitress will recite that evening's offerings, which typically include steaks, ham, seafood, and chicken dishes. Along with your entree, you will receive a pass at the lavish salad bar, a choice of fresh vegetable, potatoes (with some entrees), rolls and butter, and a beverage. And, as a special treat, you'll be served all the hot corn fritters drenched with maple syrup that you can eat. Those with an appetite after all that can choose from an assortment of tempting fresh desserts. The homemade pies rate high marks (the peanut butter streusel is particularly good), while ice creams, sherbets, parfaits, made-from-scratch angel food cake, and cobblers please others.

The inn's brightly wallpapered dining rooms with dark wood trim and baseboards provide an informal yet charming place to dine. The West Milton Inn is set in a grove of trees, and the walkways and landings behind the structure allow guests to enjoy a densely wooded ravine and a 30-foot waterfall.

The West Milton Inn is at the intersection of Rtes. 48 and 571, West Milton; (513) 698-4744. The inn is open seven days a week, 11 A.M.–10 P.M. Prices: moderate to expensive. Personal checks are accepted. Reservations are recommended.

With 165 acres and more than 6 miles of trails, the **Brukner Nature Center**'s mission is to preserve and present to the public the splendor of the outdoors. Hardwood and pine forests, ridges, and ravines—all are accessible by the center's nature trails. Visitors observe the flora and fauna while hiking by Cattail and Catface ponds and while following the banks of the Stillwater River.

From the observation platform at the center's prairie habitat you can see Indian grass, wild carrots, yellow coneflowers, roses, milkweeds, and other plants indigenous to a prairie and can occasionally catch a glimpse of the hawks, garter snakes, cottontail rabbits, deer, and ground squirrels that inhabit the area.

The "Raise to Release Program" nurtures back to health injured animals brought to Brukner. Those unable to survive in the wild are kept in the animal room on display for visitors to the center. Brukner also hosts a variety of classes and seminars on topics such as quilting, woodcarving, jewelry making, photography, beekeeping, and gardening.

The Brukner Nature Center is at 5995 Horseshoe Bend Road, off Rte. 55, west of Troy; (513) 698-6493. Trails are open during daylight hours. The exhibit building is open Monday through Saturday, 9 A.M.–5 P.M.; Sunday, 12:30–5 P.M. Admission: $1 per person ($2 per family on Sunday only).

After your nature hike, take the ten-minute drive to **Stillwater Wineries** to enjoy another of nature's bounties—fine Ohio wine. Stillwater, housed in an energy-efficient underground building, produces and serves twenty different wines, with $1.50 sample trays available for those unsure of their preference. The winery's straining and storage equipment is in the back of the building, while the bar and tasting room, with its two large fireplaces, occupies the front half of the structure. Crackers, breadsticks, and cheese are also available.

Stillwater Wineries is at 2311 West Rte. 55, west of I-75 and Troy; (513) 339-8346. Open Tuesday through Friday, 4:30–11 P.M.; Saturday, 1–11 P.M.

In 1804, for $5 an acre, John Johnston bought the 235 acres he called "Upper Pickaway Farms." John and Rachel Johnston, along with their eleven children, lived in the family farmhouse from its completion in 1815 to the 1860s. This historic farm has been restored to its appearance in 1829 and is now part of the **Piqua Historical Area.**

The farmhouse is completely furnished with pieces dating from the early 1800s. The Johnstons used the outdoor fruit kiln to dry apple slices from the farm's two orchards. One feature that attracted Johnston to this property was the flowing spring, and he built a springhouse to utilize the cool spring water to refrigerate meats, milk, and produce. Inside the two-story structure, the clear water circles a stone island in the center of the floor. Items requiring cooling were placed either on the stones or in the flowing water. The spring also provided fresh drinking water for the family. When Johnston advertised the farm for sale in 1857, he estimated the spring's output at ten gallons per minute. The second floor of the springhouse originally contained accommodations for the farm's hired help, but today holds an oak loom (c. 1750) on which rug making is demonstrated.

The Johnston's enormous double-pen log barn, constructed in 1808, is the largest log barn in Ohio. Johnston used it for his flock of 100 sheep, and the original pens and beams are still plainly visible. Other attractions at the Piqua Historical Area include canalboat rides on a restored section of the Miami and Erie Canal and an Indian museum dedicated to the tribes prevalent in Ohio from the seventeenth to mid-nineteenth centuries.

The Piqua Historical Area is located on Hardin Road east of Rte. 66, north of Piqua; (513) 773-2522. Open from Memorial Day to Labor Day, Wednesday through Saturday, 9:30 A.M.–5 P.M.; Sunday, noon–5 P.M. May be open weekends in September and October. Admission: age thirteen and above, $3.

Shelby County

Though it may surprise many Californians and New Yorkers, Ohio was the country's leading wine-producing state prior to the Civil War. That tradition continues with more than fifty wineries in operation from the Lake Erie islands to Cincinnati.

The original owners of **Vinterra Farm Winery and Vineyard**, Homer ("Bud") and Phyllis Monroe, first planted grapes in 1973. Art and Connie Muhlenkamp purchased the estate in 1985 for the same purpose—to create fine wines in the European tradition. This forty-acre farm has eleven acres of French hybrid grapes and 650 semi-dwarf apple trees. All grapes harvested here are sent to the cellar to produce estate-bottled wines. The apples provide delightful "pick-your-own" weekends for families.

Visitors to the winery sample an assortment of wines inside the spacious, Bavarian-style tasting room or on the outdoor veranda. A tasting tray offers seven small glasses of Vinterra vintages, plus French breadsticks. Cheese, crackers, summer sausage, pizzas, and other homemade appetizers are also available. Occasional steak cookouts, gourmet dinners, pig roasts, and nature walks take place throughout the year. The Muhlenkamps gladly conduct tours of their wine cellar, where 5,000 gallons are produced annually.

Vinterra Farm Winery and Vineyard is at 6505 Stoker Road, off Rte. 66 (south of Rte. 47), Houston; (513) 492-2071. From June through Labor Day, the winery is open Tuesday through Saturday, 1–10 P.M.; Sunday, 1–5 P.M. The rest of the year, Vinterra is open Friday, 5–10 P.M.; and Saturday, 1–10 P.M.

For some of the best ice cream in west central Ohio, stop by the **Sidney Dairy** for a bowl or cone of your favorite flavor. Housed in an unpretentious single-story brick building in a primarily residential section of Sidney, this dairy ice cream shop offers more than forty-eight flavors of freshly made ice cream and sherbet. And at 65¢ per dip, this may be the best ice cream value in the state.

In addition to the usual flavors, the dairy creates some innovative ones, such as old south fudge pie, pecan pie, deep-dish apple pie, plantation peach cobbler, and peanut butter ripple—all made right on the premises. The dairy's front room ice cream shop also makes delicious sundaes, banana splits, and other fountain concoctions, and ice cream packaged in cartons is ready to take home. If you have trouble finding the Sidney Dairy, ask anyone in town—the place is that popular.

The Sidney Dairy is at the intersection of North Miami and Shelby streets at 507 North Miami, Sidney; (513) 492-4300. Open Monday through Saturday, 11:30 A.M.–9:30 P.M.; Sunday, 12:30–9:30 P.M.

Logan County

The 6,000-acre Indian Lake, with its shady islands, peninsulas, and lakefront homes, attracts recreation seekers for fishing, boating, and water skiing.

With two- and three-bedroom cottages, **O'Connor's Landing**, which has been in the O'Connor family since its founding in 1904, provides family oriented accommodations at Indian Lake. The cottages ring a quiet, protected inlet. All come with modest furnishings, refrigerators, gas stoves, and pots, pans, and kitchen equipment.

O'Connor's dock handles forty-five boats, sells marine fuel, and rents canoes and fishing boats. A launching ramp is adjacent to the dock. Reservations are suggestd, since many families reserve a cottage year after year at this scenic resort.

O'Connor's Landing is just west of Rte. 117, Belle Center; (513) 842-4941. Open April through September. Rates: $45 to $55 per night, $140 to $185 per week.

Wicker Resort is another lodging option on Indian Lake. The two- and three-bedroom cottages, all in a shady section on the lakefront, are available from mid-April through October. Most guests at Wicker Resort, with its private boat dock, spend more time on the water than in the clean, simply furnished cottages. The large frame Wicker's Hotel, once a posh getaway, now stands idle, awaiting restoration.

Wicker Resort is on Orchard Island in Russells Point; (513) 843-3666. Rates: $280 to $350 per week during summer months; $180 to $250 per week during spring and fall months. Weekend rates are also available. Reservations are recommended.

Fifteen miles southeast of Indian Lake, a private park, **Zane Caverns**, offers a fascinating cavern, camping, and unique accommodations. A swift underground river eroded the eleven-million-year-old cavern in the limestone, leaving a labyrinth of caves and tunnels and unusual crystal formations. Water seeping through the rock and dripping down on limestone boulders has created the distinctive beehive crystals, and in one case, the rare cave pearls. These pure white crystal balls formed in a small pool of water around tiny pieces of rock and dust. The only other set of similar pearls in existence is in a cave in Switzerland.

Zane Caverns, with its many "rooms," splendid colors, and clear pools of 40-degree water, was discovered by a young boy in 1892 when his dog fell in a hole and dropped down into the cavern. Early visitors entered through that same hole (which is still visible from inside the cavern) and were lowered in a basket and given a kerosene lamp. In the early 1900s, these self-guided tours cost 10¢.

Today it takes about forty minutes for the guides to lead a group from one end of the cavern to the other. The tour reaches a depth of 132 feet below the surface, but various tunnels and cre-vasses shot off from the main cavern to even greater depths.

Zane Caverns is open daily from May through September, and Friday through Sunday in April and October, 10 A.M.–5 P.M. Admission: adults, $5; children (ages six–twelve), $2.50.

The cavern's 200 acres of woods, ridges, and ravines also offer camping and lodging for overnight guests. The park's only cabin, formerly the manager's residence, has two bedrooms, a large stone fireplace, kitchen facilities, pine paneling, and a screened porch. Set near the swimming pond at the edge of a heavily wooded section of the park, the cabin rents for $35 per night for two people, with each additional person over age six an extra $2.50 per night.

Zane Caverns also has a covered wagon fitted out with seats, carpeting, screens, electric lights, and a double bed for rustic sleeping outdoors. Another delightful place to rest one's head is the Eagles' Nest. Set on stilts in a heavily wooded ravine, this screened sleeping shelter contains a double bed, with a picnic table and barbecue grill adjacent. The Covered Wagon rents for $20 per night for two people; the Eagles' Nest, $22.50 per night.

Zane Caverns is on Rte. 540, 5 miles east of Bellefontaine; (513) 592-0891. Open April through October. MasterCard and Visa are accepted.

Winter recreation in Logan County is centered at **Mad River Mountain**'s ski resort, with eight slopes and trails for skiers open during the November through March season. Ski instruction and rental are offered, and the twenty-three–room lodge provides meals, your favorite beverages, and overnight accommodations after a long day on the slopes. During summer months, tennis courts and a swimming pool attract visitors to Mad River's 400 hilly, wooded acres.

Mad River Mountain is on Rte. 33, 5 miles east of Bellefontaine; (513) 599-1015.

Rural Logan County might seem an unusual place for two brothers to build a pair of castles, but that is precisely what Colonel Donn Piatt and General Abram Saunders Piatt did during the 1860s and 1870s. Members of the Piatt family came to America in 1690 from southeastern France. Donn and Abram's grandfather, Jacob Piatt, served on George Washington's staff during the Revolutionary War. Jacob's son Benjamin, after fighting in the War of 1812, purchased 1,700 acres in the Ohio Valley. It was Benjamin's sons Donn and Abram who built the two stone castles a mile apart in what is today Logan County.

Abram Piatt built the first one, patterned after Norman French castles, in 1864—**Castle Piatt Mac-A-Cheek**, named after a local Indian tribe. The three-story home (with five-story watch tower) has walls 2 feet thick made of limestone quarried and hand-chiseled on the site.

The castle has remained in the Piatt family since its construction, and all furnishings in the castle are original. The first stop on guided tours of Castle Piatt Mac-A-Cheek is the spacious drawing room, with its intricate oak, walnut, and cherry floors and splendid ash, pine, and walnut walls. Fine woodwork graces the entire castle, as do the frescoed ceilings painted by French artist Oliver Frey in 1880. These ceilings have survived a century surprisingly well, without so much as a touch up.

The castle's furnishings include horsehair-covered couches and chairs, massive carved beds, and wardrobes—some dating as far back as the Revolutionary War period. The family's antique gun collection and a private chapel, complete with altar and kneeler, are upstairs.

Down the road, Donn Piatt's Flemish-style **Castle Mac-O-Chee** (a variation of the name Mac-A-Cheek) contains an outstanding collection of European and Asiatic furnishings and art. The Piatt family lost control of the three-story, twin-spired castle in 1891, when the Colonel's widow sold the property. The Piatts re-acquired Mac-O-Chee in 1956 and restored it after it had been severely vandalized.

The Piatt Castles are on Rte. 245 2 miles east of West Liberty;

The Harding Home

(513) 465-2821. Castle Mac-A-Cheek is open April through October, daily from 11 A.M.–5 P.M. Castle Mac-O-Chee is open May through September, daily 11 A.M.–5 P.M., plus weekends in April and October. Admission charge.

Marion County

In 1890, Warren G. Harding, then twenty-five years old, and his fiancee planned and had built the dark green home at 380 Mount Vernon Avenue, Marion. From the **Harding Home**, he conducted his famous "front porch" campaign in 1920 and won the presidency. The Harding years in the White House were turbulent ones—his administration was racked by scandals, including the infamous "Teapot Dome" incident. Harding died in San Francisco in 1923, without completing his term of office.

The eldest son of a doctor, Harding was born in Blooming Grove, Ohio, on Nov. 2, 1865. After working as a printer's appren-

115

tice, he bought the *Marion Daily Star* at the age of nineteen. In 1891, he married Florence Kling DeWolfe, daughter of one of Marion's wealthiest and most prominent Republicans, on the stairway of the home they had designed. Harding's election to the Ohio Senate in 1899, as lieutenant governor of Ohio in 1903, and to the United States Senate in 1914 laid the groundwork for his successful presidential campaign in 1920. Harding used the large front porch of his home, the porch he had expanded in 1900, to speak to the 600,000 voters who traveled to Marion in the summer of 1920 to hear the acclaimed oratory of the Republican candidate.

Inside the entryway sits the small wooden desk where Harding sat on election night reading the latest telegraphed election returns. Nearly all the furnishings and accessories in the Harding home are exactly as the Hardings left them when they went to Washington in 1921. Many of the art objects collected by the Hardings on their three trips to Europe are there, and so is the hat worn by the twenty-ninth president at his inauguration. The small building behind the Harding residence, which served as the press headquarters during the 1920 campaign, now is a museum.

The Harding Home is at 380 Mount Vernon Avenue, Marion; (614) 387-9630. Open Memorial Day to Labor Day, Wednesday through Saturday, 9:30 A.M.–5 P.M.; Sunday, noon–5 P.M. May be open weekends in September and October. Admission: adults, $1.50; children (ages six to twelve), $1.

Not far from the Harding Home are the ten-acre grounds containing the **Warren G. Harding Memorial**. Constructed in 1927 of Georgia white marble, the 52-foot-tall memorial surrounds the graves of President and Mrs. Harding (she died in 1924, a year after her husband). Emerald pearl labrador granite tombstones cover the graves of the Hardings, who were buried here on Dec. 21, 1927. The careful rows of maple trees on the grounds form the shape of a Latin cross.

The Harding Memorial is at the corner of Rte. 423 and Vernon Heights Blvd., Marion; open daylight hours; no admission charge.

Marion offers visitors another intriguing museum: **The Stengel-True Museum**. Judge Ozias Bowen built this three-story mansion in 1864 at a cost of $20,000. Bowen arrived in Marion from New York in 1828 and married Miss Lydia Baker, the daughter of Eber Baker, the founder of Marion. Judge Bowen's grandson, Henry A. True, made a provision in his will establishing the museum, and a local optometrist, Dr. Frederick Stengel, contributed many of the collections displayed at Stengel-True.

A wonderful old Regina music box plays waltzes (for a nickel). The front parlor contains a grand piano that once belonged to Florence Kling Harding and one of the ornate marble fireplaces found throughout the museum. Displays include collections of rare and antique guns, all types of early lamps and lighting instruments (from candles to kerosene fixtures), and a wall full of antique clocks (next to a case loaded with old pocket watches).

Pioneer antiques dominate the upper floors—spinning wheels, yarn winders, dough pans, hay forks, and a butter churn. A small staircase on the third floor leads up to the rooftop cupola, with a splendid 360-degree view of Marion.

The Stengel-True Historical Museum is at the corner of South State Street and Washington Avenue (504 South State Street), Marion; (614) 387-6140. Open Saturday and Sunday, 1–4:30 P.M. No admission charge.

Auglaize County

At 10:56:20 Eastern Daylight Time on July 20, 1969, Neil Armstrong became the first man to step onto the lunar surface. "That's one small step for a man—one giant leap for mankind," crackled Armstrong's first radio transmission from Tranquility Base, as he accomplished the goal set by John Kennedy in the early 1960s. It was less than seventy years earlier that Dayton's Wright brothers had conquered powered flight over the sands of Kitty Hawk—from the first successful aircraft to lunar exploration in a little more than six decades.

The **Neil Armstrong Air and Space Museum** in Wapakoneta celebrates the achievements of local boy Armstrong and other Ohioans who contributed to the field of aviation. A NASA F5D Skylancer aircraft flown by Armstrong in the early 1960s greets visitors, and from the Skylancer you simply follow the runway lights to the entrance of the futuristic exhibit building.

Sketches, models, and photographs trace the history of manned flight, from the earliest use of balloons to powered aircraft and space travel. The bright yellow, single engine Aeronca propeller plane flown by Armstrong at age sixteen and his Gemini Eight space capsule span his accomplishments as an aviator.

Other exhibits include spacesuits from both Gemini and Apollo missions, a Jupiter rocket engine, and not-particularly-tempting packets of astronaut space food. One video projection room continuously shows marvelous footage of American astronauts from various Apollo missions walking, hopping, jumping, and driving on the lunar surface.

The Neil Armstrong Air and Space Museum is at I-75 and Bellefontaine Road, Wapakoneta; (419) 738-8811. Open March through November, Monday through Saturday, 9:30 A.M.–5 P.M.; Sunday noon–5 P.M. Admission: adults, $2; children (ages six to twelve), $1.

Mercer County

One location on the Wabash River was the site of both one of the worst defeats and one of the most important victories for American troops battling the Indians in the 1790s. Indian warriors led by Little Turtle and Blue Jacket caught General Arthur St. Clair's forces in a surprise attack on Nov. 4, 1791, killing or wounding three quarters of the soldiers.

But two years after St. Clair's defeat, General "Mad Anthony" Wayne picked that spot on the Wabash to construct a fort consisting of four blockhouses connected by log stockade walls. Each blockhouse measured 20 feet square, and Wayne's troops finished **Fort Recovery** in less than a week. When the Indians attacked on the morning of June 30, 1794, Wayne's forces prevailed, setting the stage for the general's final victory over the Indians at Fallen Timbers on Aug. 20, 1794, and the signing of the Treaty of Greene Ville in 1795.

Visitors to Fort Recovery inspect the two reconstructed blockhouses and view artifacts from the original fort in the two-story stone museum. These artifacts include an army issue felling ax, bottles, a skillet handle, and bone-handled knives and forks. The museum has other items used in battle here nearly two centuries ago, such as howitzer shells, cannon balls, grape shot, and parts of muskets and pistols.

One exhibit explains the construction of Fort Recovery, where 13-foot logs with one end axed to a point were placed on end in 3-foot-deep trenches to form the stockade walls. A gap approximately every 6 feet allowed the fort's defenders to point their rifles through the wall and fire on attackers. Other displays include mannequins of an army sergeant and an Indian brave clothed in their respective 1794 battle uniforms, a collection of muskets and military swords from the 1860s, plus Indian artifacts from Mercer County such as tomahawks, leather goods, and arrowheads.

Fort Recovery is near the intersection of Rtes. 49 and 119, Fort Recovery; (419) 375-4649. Open May 1 to Labor Day, Tuesday through Saturday, 1–5 P.M.; Sunday, noon–5 P.M. Also open on weekends in May and September. Admission: adults, $1; children, 50¢.

Allen County

Lima residents boast of having one of the best county museums in the state—the **Allen County Museum**—and it is. Two floors contain hundreds of items in a modern, brick building. Its pioneer kitchen contains old-fashioned butter stamps, molds, and churns, while the pioneer bedroom has a corn husk mattress on a primitive wooden bed. The mother of the Haller twins (Kathern and Sophie) rocked her infants on the rare double cradle bench during their first year in 1852.

The museum has collected a variety of wagons and buggies, including a covered wagon and a hearse, as well as antique cars such as a magnificent 1910 REO touring car. Downstairs features a number of muskets and pistols and all manner of Indian items including arrowheads, beads, ornate Hopi dolls and masks, pottery, blankets, and a large ribbed canoe. A nineteenth-century doctor's office and a general store are completely stocked with items typical of the era.

One unusual item is the 1903 Kodak "mugging" camera, used by the Lima police department at the turn of the century (plus sample mugshots demonstrating the policemen's photographic abilities). Other collections include rocks, fossils, and minerals found in the county and a group of antique farm implements.

Next to the museum is the Log House, furnished with primitive pioneer possessions, and the MacDonnell House, a Victorian mansion renowned for its handsome woodwork, big game trophies, and period pieces.

The Allen County Museum is at 620 West Market Street, Lima; (419) 222-9426. Open from Tuesday through Sunday, 1:30–5 P.M. No admission charge.

Wyandot County

Richard Hendricks purchased his dream in 1963—the 650-foot **Indian Trail Caverns** he had first visited as a child. Once called the Wyandot Indian Caverns, this bit of underground history first opened in 1927, but closed ten years later. Hendricks, the postmaster in nearby Vanlue, worked nights and weekends whenever the weather would permit, clearing glacial debris from the floor of the caverns, and reopened them in 1975.

Acidic water seeping through the 400-million-year-old rock created the caverns. The formation of the caverns was particularly rapid (in geological time) when this part of Ohio was under a warm, shallow ocean. In fact, Indian Trail was part of a reef millions of years ago. Advancing glaciers dumped sandy debris on the floor of the caverns, and Hendricks has removed much of it to increase the height of the caverns. In addition to the 650 feet now open to the public, Hendricks believes another 400 feet will eventualy be passable, plus whatever new tunnels further excavation uncovers.

Hendricks has learned a great deal about his caverns from the many geologists and archeologists who have studied the formation, and he shares his knowledge with those who tour the caves. Smoke-stained walls and ceilings, in addition to artifacts discovered here, indicate that prehistoric man lived in the caverns, taking advantage of the year-round 52-degree temperature. Indian Trail has two skylights open to the surface and a natural stone ladder that Indians may have used to go in and out of this unique geological formation. Hendricks delights in pointing out dozens of natural rock sculptures which seem to form shapes such as Abe Lincoln's face and a wolf's head.

Indian Trail Caverns is on Rte. 568, 4 miles northwest of Carey; (419) 387-7015, 387-7773. Open May through September, Tuesday through Sunday, 1–6 P.M. or by appointment. Admission: adults, $4.50; children, $3.

The United States government constructed a saw and gristmill for Ohio's Wyandot Indians in 1820 in gratitude for their support during the War of 1812. The mill was on the Sandusky River, and government-appointed millers ground flour and cornmeal for the Wyandot reservation until the Indians were relocated to Kansas in 1843, putting the mill out of operation.

A second mill was built 300 feet downstream from the first in 1861 and operated until 1941. This mill had a reputation for particularly good stone ground buckwheat and cornmeal and has since become the country's first museum of milling—**Indian Mill State Memorial**.

The museum includes a detailed explanation of the four types of mill waterwheels: the overshot, undershot, breast, and horizontal wheels. Exhibits explain the history of gristmills and sawmills and their importance to early Ohio settlements. Perhaps the most intriguing feature of the museum is the working model of a water turbine mill. This model demonstrates the complex system of "flights" which transported grain and milled meal from floor to floor in the mill—from its entry down a chute to the grinding stones on the lower level to the upper floors for sifting, separating, and sacking. Outside the mill, a three-acre park across the river bridge is a tranquil and picturesque spot for a picnic or just relaxing.

Indian Mill State Memorial is on County Road 47, off Rte. 67 northeast of Upper Sandusky; (419) 294-3349. Open June through October, Thursday through Saturday, 9:30 A.M.–5 P.M.; Sunday, 1–6 P.M. Admission: adults, $1; children, 50¢.

Richland County

More and more travelers are choosing bed and breakfast lodgings, in reaction to expensive, impersonal hotels and motels. One of the nicest such accommodations in Ohio opened in 1981 in an 1863 Victorian home—the **Frederick Fitting House**. Built by a prominent Bellville businessman, Frederick Fitting (he brought the railroad to Bellville), the home has three distinctive bedrooms for travelers: the Colonial Room with its canopy bed and colonial coverlet, the Victorian Room, which has an ornate brass bed, and the Shaker Room with original Shaker pieces. The three guest rooms are on the second floor and share a bath; the owners live in attached carriage house. They bought the Fitting House in 1980 and have extensively renovated the property. The house, now painted a creamy beige and trimmed in peach and rust, occupies a corner lot in a quiet residential neighborhood with many tall trees.

Ohio country antiques furnish the first floor, and a fire burns in the fireplace all winter long. The exquisite dining room, with its hand-stenciled walls, is the focal point of the home, and here the Sowashes serve a complimentary breakfast of homemade breads,

The Frederick Fitting House

pastries, fresh fruit, and coffee. Many guests are drawn to the area by the two nearby ski resorts (Clear Fork in Butler and Snow Trails in Mansfield) during winter months.

The Frederick Fitting House is at 72 Fitting Avenue, Bellville; (419) 886-4283. Rates: $40 to $50 per night. Reservations and a deposit are required.

Humphrey Bogart and Lauren Bacall married and honeymooned on a farm near Lucas, Ohio? Unlikely as that might seem, it did happen on May 21, 1945, at **Malabar**, the 915-acre farm of Pulitzer-winning novelist Louis Bromfield. Bromfield was born in nearby Mansfield in 1896 and graduated from Mansfield Senior High School. Though he studied agriculture at Cornell and journalism at Columbia, this prominent author and screenplay writer never received a college degree.

After driving ambulances in World War I, Bromfield published his first novel, *The Green Bay Tree*, in 1925, launching a literary career that would produce thirty-three books over the next thirty-three years, as well as a number of screenplays. While dedicated to his writing, Bromfield never lost his interest in agriculture. In 1939, when the outbreak of World War II forced Bromfield and his family to flee France, he began searching Ohio for suitable farm acreage to practice the conservation techniques he had learned from his grandfather and French farmers. He found Malabar or, more accurately, created Malabar (which means "beautiful valley" in an Indian dialect), by purchasing four adjacent farms in the lush rolling hills of Richland County. Saving only four rooms of the original farmhouse, Bromfield added twenty-eight others, including nine bedrooms, six full baths and four half baths, to produce the airy rambling estate where he entertained family and friends.

Among the many visitors to Malabar were Hollywood celebrities such as William Powell, Errol Flynn, Dorothy Lamour, and Shirley Temple—all friends of Bromfield's from his work in motion pictures. Bromfield explained his innovative "grass farming" method of agriculture to them, a system of planting grasses in critical areas to arrest soil erosion and reinvigorate the earth. Bromfield distrusted the effects on the soil of using every available acre for grain production; instead he cultivated only enough acreage to support his dairy operation.

The Bromfield home is furnished exactly as it was when the family lived here, with many of the pieces brought back from France in 1939. Bromfield also imported the bright wallpapers from France, and all the oak floors and walnut doors are original. Two Grandma Moses paintings hang in the house, and, because of Bromfield's love of the outdoors, every room on the first floor has an outside door. Bromfield had the twenty-nine–drawer desk in his study custom built, only to discover he was unhappy with the way it "felt." Bromfield actually worked at a card table behind the desk.

The family's boxer dogs were important members of the household, and the doors of the house were equipped with special door latches that the dogs could open, giving them free run of Malabar. In addition to guided tours of the house, self-guided tours of the barns, chicken coop, smokehouse, and the farm's active dairy operation are also offered. Cross-country skiing is popular at the farm in the winter, with rental equipment available.

Malabar Farm is west of Rte. 603 off Pleasant Valley Road,

south of Lucas; (419) 892-2784. Open daily year-round, except major holidays. No charge for farm tours or wagon rides; tours of the house cost $1.25 for adults, 50¢ for children ages six to eighteen.

Just down the road from Malabar Farm is a former stagecoach stop on the old Cleveland-Marietta line called the **Malabar Inn**. David Schrack and his sons, attracted to this location because of the rapidly flowing spring (later called Niman Spring), built the inn in 1820. The inn had deteriorated badly when Louis Bromfield acquired it in the late 1930s, but Bromfield renovated the structure and used it to house the overflow of guests visiting Malabar. Bromfield also took advantage of the springhouse next to the inn, using the cold water flowing through the sandstone troughs to cool the organic produce sold at his roadside market.

The Malabar Inn today serves fine country fare in the brick two-story building, which now has a large deck on three sides. Dinner selections include rainbow trout, smoked Ohio ham, steaks, roast top round of beef, and pan-fried calves' liver with bacon. One of the more intriguing entrees is the rouladen bourgignonne—slices of lean beef filled with a mixture of ham, ground beef, and herbs, rolled and baked in a burgundy wine sauce. Diners may choose from a half dozen daily specials such as fresh bay scallops sauteed in wine sauce, veal parmigiana, and pan-fried trout.

For lunch, there are salads, sandwiches, homemade soups, and specialty entrees. One dining room is elegantly paneled and trimmed in white; the other features bright wallpaper. Both have a Williamsburg flair, potted plants, and plenty of windows for enjoying the tall trees around the inn. The breads and desserts at Malabar are made from scratch, and the rich cheesecake with fresh strawberries is particularly good.

The Malabar Inn is on Pleasant Valley Road, just west of Rte. 603, south of Lucas; (419) 938-5205. Open March through December, Sunday through Tuesday, 11 A.M.–8 P.M.; Wednesday through Saturday, 11 A.M.–9 P.M. Prices: lunch, inexpensive to moderate; dinner, moderate to expensive. MasterCard and Visa are accepted.

The late Charles Kelly King, chairman of the board of Mansfield's Ohio Brass Company, spent $400,000 building and furnishing his palatial French Provincial estate in 1926—an estate now dedicated to the study and display of gardening, horticulture, bird study, and related subjects and called **Kingwood Center**.

King joined Ohio Brass in 1893, working his way through the ranks from chief engineer to sales manager, and later from vice president and president to chairman. After his death at age eighty-four in 1952, his will established an endowment for the development and perpetual maintenance of Kingwood. Two of the three floors of the mansion are open to the public. Perhaps the most impressive room is the formal dining room, with its hand-painted French wallpaper, delicate crystal chandelier, and antique chairs and table—a room that any monarch would proudly claim. The mansion also houses an extensive library on horticulture, landscaping, and related topics.

The grounds of the estate include twelve distinct gardens, each designed and arranged by the staff. The center plants 45,000 tulips each year, with the peak blooming season for these during the first two weeks in May. The paths also take you past Kingwood's collections of trees, shrubs, and ferns, and nature trails allow you to enjoy the abundant wildflowers. A variety of ducks and ornamental birds freely roam the grounds, and 130 species of native birds have been sighted on the premises.

Kingwood Center is at 900 Park Avenue West (Rte. 430), in Mansfield; (419) 522-0211. Gardens and nature areas are open daily, 8 A.M.–sundown. Kingwood Hall is open Tuesday through Saturday, 9 A.M.–5 P.M.; Sunday (Easter through October only), 1:30–4:30 P.M. No admission charge.

Off the Beaten Path in Northwest Ohio

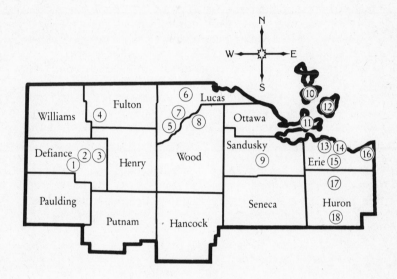

1. AuGlaize Village
2. Fort Defiance
3. Independence Dam State Park
4. Sauder Farm and Craft Village/ Barn Restaurant
5. Columbian House/Bluebird Passenger Train/Grand Rapids
6. Wildwood Preserve Metropark
7. Fallen Timbers State Memorial
8. Fort Meigs
9. Rutherford B. Hayes Presidential Center
10. South Bass Island (Put-in-Bay)
11. Mon Ami Restaurant/East Harbor

State Park/Island House/ Greenhouse Restaurant/Hotel Lakeside/Marblehead Lighthouse/Poor Richards Inn
12. Kelleys Island
13. Cedar Point
14. Twine House/Wileswood Country Store
15. Edison Museum and Birthplace/ Milan Inn
16. Vermilion
17. Firelands Museum
18. Historic Lyme Village/Mad River & NKP Railroad Society Museum

Northwest Ohio

Defiance County

Surrounded by cornfields in the plains of northwest Ohio is a unique historical village—**AuGlaize Village**. Seventeen reconstructed or restored buildings (c. 1860 to 1920) have been gathered from the area and provide visitors with a glimpse of life a century ago in this flat farming region of the state. Self-guided tours of AuGlaize allow you to explore at your own pace.

In Doctor Cameron's office, built in 1874 in Jewell, there are old medical journals and catalogs advertising medical products such as foot and ankle braces and the "Harvard Physician's Chair" rural doctors used for surgery, adjusting it to one of dozens of positions depending on the particular procedure to be performed. Dr. Cameron owned one of these chairs, and it is in the back room of his office.

The Chapel of Crosses Church, which the congregation of Saint John's Lutheran Church in Sherwood built in 1875, is a one-room, frame structure containing an antique wooden pump organ. The Story and Clark Company of Chicago manufactured this ornately carved instrument in 1892.

The Sherry School has textbooks from the mid-1800s, including McGuffey's *Eclectic Spelling Book*, teacher Mable Carroll's attendance records from the 1882 school year, and a student's certificate of promotion from 1896. The mailboxes in the front room of the old post office from Mark Centre still have mail in them—a 1906 copy of the *Saturday Evening Post* and a postcard dated 1899 notifying a Defiance man that he owes the Farmer Mutual Fire Protection Association another 25¢ on his insurance policy.

Other restored buildings include a completely equipped 1903 dentist's office (containing some grisly-looking instruments), the Ayersville Telephone Company with its old-fashioned switchboard and telephones, a blacksmith's shop, and the Minsel Barber Shop.

AuGlaize Village's two museums hold a varied collection of pioneer items. One building has an extensive assortment of antique farm implements, such as an elaborate, horse-drawn straw baler, and numerous fruit and tobacco presses. Also in the museum is a rare 1919 Defiance Motor Company truck. This local auto and truck manufacturer assembled vehicles for six years until the company failed in 1925. For military buffs, a separate building contains military equipment and hardware, including Civil War uniforms, cannons and mortars, and a variety of pistols and muskets (including a 1763 "Brown Bess" flintlock).

Throughout its season, AuGlaize Village hosts special Events Days, such as the annual Harvest Demonstration and the Johnny Appleseed Festival. Craft experts show the old-fashioned way to dip candles and weave rugs and other pioneer skills. The admission charge to the village on Events Days is slightly higher than the regular rates.

AuGlaize Village is south of Rte. 24 on Krouse Road, 3 miles west of Defiance; (419) 784-0107. The village is open from Memorial Day through mid-October, Saturday and Sunday, 10 A.M.–5 P.M. AuGlaize Village is open weekends only in September and October. Admission: adults, $2; children and senior citizens, $1.

A quiet residential neighborhood in nearby Defiance is the site of a former fortification that played a significant role in this region's history. The bluff at the confluence of the Maumee and Auglaize rivers was where General "Mad Anthony" Wayne's American troops built **Fort Defiance** in 1794. Wayne launched his campaign against the Indians and British in the area from this fort, which consisted of four blockhouses and a tall stockade fence around the perimeter. It was erected in five weeks, and General Wayne, admiring the completed fortification, is reported to have said, "I defy the British, the Indians and all the devils in hell to take it!" Upon hearing that, a fellow officer suggested, "Then call it Fort Defiance."

It was from here that Wayne's forces marched against the Indians, defeating them at the Battle of Fallen Timbers. Two cannons, one facing each river, are all that remain of the fort today. When you stand on that hill, however, at the junction of those two great rivers, the strategic importance of this spot is readily apparent.

The Fort Defiance Memorial is at the end of Washington Avenue, in Defiance. It is open daylight hours, and no admission is charged.

East of Defiance in nearby Independence is another historic site. **Independence Dam State Park** is a long, narrow green space between the swift Maumee River and a now-idle section of the old Miami and Erie Canal. This canal, which was built during the 1820s, 1830s, and 1840s, connected Toledo (and Lake Erie)

129

with Cincinnati (and the Ohio River). As part of the canal construction boom in Ohio early in the nineteenth century, the Miami and Erie provided cheap transportation for goods and new
settlers, stimulating the economic development of the region.
Nevertheless, by as early as the 1850s, the speed and flexibility of
the railroad signaled the beginning of the end of the canal era.

Independence Dam was built to divert water from the river to
the canal, and this section of the Miami and Erie holds water to
this day. The massive wooden gates of Lock 13 at the entrance to
the park are the only such gates still in existence on this canal. In
sharp contrast to the boom years, today the banks are overgrown, and the former towpaths have been erased by time.

Visitors to the park can take advantage of the hiking trails,
picnic areas, and primitive campsites. Fishing and boating are
popular on the wide Maumee River, and the park has boat
launching ramps.

Independence Dam State Park is on Rte. 424, 3 miles east of
Defiance; (419) 784-3263. Open year-round, no admission charge.

Fulton County

For more than two decades, Erie J. Sauder has had an interest
in the history of northwest Ohio. First he collected antique woodworking tools to display for his customers at the Sauder Woodworking Company. From woodworking equipment, his collection
expanded to include farm tools and household items used in this
section of the state in the late 1800s. These were the humble
beginnings of the **Sauder Farm and Craft Village** near Archbold. This part of the state was one of the last to be settled, due to
the 2,000-square-mile Black Swamp. Only after massive drainage
and land reclamation in the 1850s was this unhealthy muck
transformed into fertile farmland.

Sauder Farm and Craft Village is a well-organized, carefully
presented living museum. The village actually consists of three
major areas: the restored farmstead, the pioneer craft village, and
the museum.

Period pieces furnish the farmhouse, which was built in 1860.
Wood cooking and heating stoves, rope spring beds, and a
wooden pump organ are typical items found in the two-story
house. Costumed guides in each room explain the history and
demonstrate the utility of the furnishings and equipment—how

to use a hand-crank apple peeler, for instance. The last stop on the farmhouse tour is the root cellar, where the farm family stored its fruits and vegetables during winter months. Horses, sheep, turkeys, ducks, geese, and chickens roam the farmyard, and the miniature horses are a particular favorite of the children. Candle-dipping demonstrations also take place in the yard.

The craft village consists of a cluster of rustic buildings, set in a circle, each housing an expert in a particular craft. Brooms are made the old-fashioned way in the broom shop and are available for purchase, while the blacksmith busily forges candleholders, ladles, gates, and railings. One of the most popular shops belongs to Mark Matthews, the village glassblower. Taking 2,000-degree glass from the bottom of the furnace, Mark adds color chips to the clear glass, then blows and hand shapes this soft, hot glass into beautiful pitchers, vases, and paperweights. As with the other craftsmen in the village, Mark explains each step of the process. Other demonstrations at Sauder's include woodcarving, pottery throwing, coopering, spinning, weaving, tinsmithing, and basketry.

The village museum contains an impressive collection of tools, machinery, and household items used by early settlers in this region. A large number of old farm wagons, buggies, and carts are on display, as are farm craft tools, such as woodworking tools, and farm implements including an 1886 potato digger and an 1860 cultivator. The museum's Conestoga wagon, first designed in 1755 in Conestoga Valley, Pennsylvania, once transported newcomers to the area. Countless meat grinders, butter churns, wood-burning stoves, and foot-powered sewing machines fill this vast exhibit space. A quilting demonstration also takes place there, and finished quilts are sold.

Sauder Farm and Craft Village is located on Rte. 2, northeast of Archbold; (419) 446-2541. Open from late April through October, Monday through Saturday, 9:30 A.M.–5 P.M.; Sunday, 1–5:00 P.M. Admission: adults, $5; children (ages six to eighteen), $2.50. MasterCard and Visa are accepted.

If you have worked up an appetite touring the Sauder Farm Museum and Craft Village, stop in next door at Erie Sauder's **Barn Restaurant**. This restaurant is housed in an actual poplar barn, which was originally built in 1875 2 miles northeast of its present location. Sauder saved the barn from being razed and had it moved in 1974.

Country cooking is the order of the day at this restaurant,

which serves family-style dinners of chicken, ham, and beef. Or, if you prefer, menu items include a selection of steaks, shrimp, and perch. The menu also offers a variety of sandwiches and salads. There are always two fresh soups warming in the large pots, including unusual ones such as Kneppley soup—a ham broth with dough drops. A generous salad bar is loaded with just about every type of salad imaginable, plus a myriad of salad fixings.

The exposed rough beams of this structure, the antique farm implements mounted on the walls, and the period costumes worn by the waitresses all enhance the rustic atmosphere of the Barn Restaurant. All breads and pastries at the restaurant are made fresh daily at the Doughbox bakery, which is next door.

The Barn Restaurant is at the Sauder Farm and Craft Village on Rte. 2, northeast of Archbold; (419) 445-2231. Open Monday through Saturday, 11 A.M.–8 P.M.; Sunday buffet, 11 A.M.–2 P.M. (The Doughbox bakery is open Monday through Saturday, 10 A.M.–5 P.M.) Prices: inexpensive to moderate. MasterCard and Visa are accepted.

Lucas County

The Maumee River town of Waterville has a fine restaurant in a historic three-story building—the **Columbian House**. Painted yellow with white trim, the Columbian House was built as a hotel and tavern in 1828 by Jack Pray, the founder of Waterville. He insisted on black walnut for all the doors and woodwork in his hotel, which served as the center of activity in Waterville for decades. (There was even a jail on the second floor at one time, used to hold prisoners being brought to the courthouse in Maumee.) The third-floor ballroom measures 20 feet by 60 feet and has fourteen carved poplar windows and 2-inch-thick white ash floors.

The first part of the twentieth century was not kind to the Columbian House, and the inn was even abandoned for a time. In 1927, however, a Toledo antique dealer bought the building and began its restoration. The next owner, the late Ethel Arnold of Findlay, purchased the structure in 1943, and, after further restoration, opened it as a restaurant in 1948. Her son and daughter-in-law now operate the Columbian House, which is listed on the National Register of Historic Places.

A large fireplace dominates the entry room, which is furnished

The Columbian House

with a comfortable couch and matching chairs. This room has the dark hardwood floors found on the entire first floor, and handsome antiques are scattered throughout. Each of the downstairs dining rooms has its own color scheme—in one, cool greens; in another, pale reds. Weather permitting, the many windows in the dining rooms are opened, allowing a fresh evening breeze to drift through the candle-lit dining areas. The second-floor bedrooms of this former inn, while not available for lodging, are furnished with period pieces and left open for visitors to admire.

After your favorite cocktail, it's time to choose from the offerings on the dinner menu, which includes baked ham in orange sauce, roast chicken and dressing, your choice of steaks, and roast prime rib. Seafood lovers can select shrimp curry over rice, red snapper amandine, or Alaskan king crab, among others. Along with vegetables, potatoes, tossed salad, and fresh bread, all

133

entrees are served with a tasty side dish—the Columbian House tomato pudding. This unusual treat is a sweet tomato concoction, served warm.

A dozen different desserts, including brownies a la mode and double chocolate mousse pie, tempt those still hungry after the generous entrees. Lunch is also served at the Columbian House, with the menu loaded with salads, soups, and sandwiches and luncheon entrees such as chicken a la king and seafood Newburg.

The Columbian House is at 3 North River Road, in Waterville; (419) 878-3006. Open Tuesday through Saturday, lunch from 11:30 A.M. to 2 P.M., dinner from 6 to 9 P.M. Closed in January. Prices: lunch, inexpensive; dinner, moderate to expensive. Visa, MasterCard, and American Express are accepted.

Before or after your meal at the Columbian House, you may want to take the scenic train ride that rolls along the tracks of the famed "Nickel Plate Road"—tracks of the Toledo, Lake Erie and Western Railway. The **Bluebird Passenger Train** meanders through the Ohio countryside and across a magnificent 900-foot bridge over the Maumee River at Grand Rapids. Trains on display at the Waterville station include a Baldwin 0-6-0 switcher, a 1908 Porter saddletank switcher, a 1946 Pullman sleeper, and a World War II Pullman troop sleeper.

The Bluebird Passenger Train is operated by the Toledo, Lake Erie & Western Railway and Museum, a non-profit group dedicated to the preservation and operation of railroad equipment, Box 168, Waterville; (419) 878-1177. The train operates weekends, May through October, with some scheduled week-day runs in summer. Group reservations are accepted, and are recommended in October when the leaves are colorful.

Lucas County is also the location of one of the state's most scenic parks—**Wildwood Preserve Metropark**. These 460 acres of lush natural beauty, with hardwood forests, ravines, meadows, and the serene Ottawa River, contain wildlife such as deer, fox, mink, muskrat, opossum, and raccoon. Owls, hawks, and pheasant nest here, and wildflowers such as bittercress, buttercups, and wild hyacinth are abundant.

The four primary hiking trails allow visitors to explore the sand dunes along the high ridge and the cottonwood and sycamore trees in the river flood plain. The prairie trail leads hikers through one of the last tall grass prairie remnants in the state, where some of the grasses reach a height of 10 feet.

The elegant Manor House, a Georgian colonial brick mansion, is nestled in a clearing and surrounded by deep, cool woods. This stately former residence has twenty-two rooms, with guided tours offered Wednesday through Sunday from noon to 5 P.M. Other facilities in the park include picnic tables, barbecue grills, shelter houses, and playground equipment.

Wildwood Preserve Metropark is at 5100 West Central Avenue (Rte. 120), east of I-475 and west of downtown Toledo; (419) 535-3050. Open daily, 7 A.M.–dark, no admission charge.

On Aug. 20, 1794, General "Mad Anthony" Wayne's army engaged an Indian war party led by Chief Little Turtle at the battleground known as Fallen Timbers, so called because a tornado felled a grove of trees here. **Fallen Timbers State Memorial** is today, almost two centuries after the battle, a peaceful reminder of that pivotal conflict—a conflict that shaped the future of Ohio's settlement by whites from the east. Wayne's defeat of the Indians here, on a bluff above the north bank of the Maumee River, led to the signing of the Treaty of Greene Ville in 1795, under which the Indians surrendered their claims to most of Ohio.

Turkey Foot Rock, a large boulder at Fallen Timbers, is the subject of Indian lore. According to legend, Chief Turkey Foot of the Ottawa tribe stood at this rock to rally his warriors against General Wayne's troops. The chief was later killed on this spot, and for years after the battle, Ottawa braves would come to Turkey Foot Rock and offer tobacco to the Great Spirit for their deceased leader.

Fallen Timbers State Memorial is on Rte. 24, west of Maumee. Open daylight hours; no admission charge.

A friendly rivalry between Gilead (now Grand Rapids) and Providence—just across the Maumee River—lasted for generations. The Howard family settled at the site of Grand Rapids in 1822, attracted to the location by the great natural beauty and the potential for commerce, thanks to the river.

On the other side of the Maumee, Peter Manor constructed a sawmill in 1822, and Providence took an early lead as the center of development for the area. That original sawmill, along with a small gristmill, was razed to make room for the Miami and Erie Canal.

In 1846, a much larger mill went up, and one hundred and forty years later, the **Isaac Ludwig Mill** still operates, if only for demonstration purposes. Most of the mill's equipment is more than seventy-five years old, and some exists from pre–Civil War days. River water diverted to a canal falls through two turbines, creating a combined force of 230 horsepower.

The canal era in this part of Ohio peaked in the 1850s, and when the railroad arrived here, it arrived in Gilead, renamed Grand Rapids, shifting commerce back across the river. An 1848 fire nearly wiped out Providence, and the great cholera epidemic of 1854 took a particularly heavy toll in the town, which today consists of only the mill, a church, and one lone home.

Although the Isaac Ludwig Mill survived the fire of 1848, a blaze a century later, in 1940, destroyed the top floors of this historic structure. The mill bears the name of its second owner, who acquired it in 1865. Isaac Ludwig died in 1906 and is buried in the township cemetery at Mount Pleasant.

Carefully restored and listed on the National Register of Historic Places, Isaac Ludwig Mill today offers a glimpse of Ohio's past. The mill produced flour, meal, and livestock feed commercially until the 1940 fire, and it continues to grind corn into cornmeal and wheat into flour as it has for decades. Visitors not only observe the art of water-powered milling but they also may purchase the results. Water power also drives drills and saws, and demonstrations of lumber being cut take place occasionally. Even the mill's electric power comes from water spinning turbines and a 1910 vintage alternator.

Isaac Ludwig Mill is on Rte. 24, across the Maumee River from Grand Rapids; (419) 832-8934. Open Saturday, 10 A.M.–4 P.M.; Sunday, 10 A.M.–6 P.M.; May through October. Also open Wednesday, Thursday, and Friday, 10 A.M.–4 P.M.; June through September. Milling and craft demonstrations on Sundays, 1–4 P.M. No admission charge.

Wood County

After your mill tour, come across the river to charming Grand Rapids, a town that has overcome considerable adversity. Fire destroyed nearly every building at one time or another during its century and a half history, and spring flooding has done serious damage, especially the floods of 1903 and 1913. As recently as 1957, flood waters filled downtown in a mere five minutes, sending residents scrambling to rooftops.

Serious restoration of Grand Rapids began in 1975, and what started slowly has picked up momentum, with most structures now in pristine condition. And special events throughout the year, from the spring flood watch, which attracts thousands to view the surging power of the scenic Maumee, to the October Applebutter Fest, add to the town's interest.

LaRoes Restaurant serves hearty food and relaxing drinks in its restaurant and tavern year-round. Housed in a building dating from the 1890s, this eye- and appetite-pleasing establishment is a local favorite. Tiffany lamps, hanging plants, bentwood chairs, and exposed brick walls create a nostalgic atmosphere. The works of artist Bill Kulhman, who grew up here and now lives in Whitehouse, Ohio, adorn the walls of the restaurant and tavern. He uses oil, pencil, chalk, and watercolor to produce his renderings of past and current residents of the area. And in a town so dominated by a river and its many floods, I suppose it's not surprising to find that the tavern features water-level indicators from some of the floods that have filled the place—water was 4 feet deep in here in 1959!

Owner David LaRoe presents casual dining and straightforward recipes at his eatery. A wide selection of soups, sandwiches, and salads awaits hungry explorers, as do dinners ranging from country ribs and steaks to frog legs and blackened red fish.

LaRoes is located on Front Street (they don't even bother with street numbers in this small town!), Grand Rapids; (419) 832-3082. Open 8 A.M.–8 P.M., Sunday through Thursday; 8 A.M.–10 P.M., Friday and Saturday; year-round. Prices: lunches, inexpensive to moderate; dinners, moderate to expensive. Personal checks are accepted.

Along Front Street in Grand Rapids are a number of unusual shops, perfect for browsing. The 100-year-old **Olde Gilead Country Store** is brimming with candles, fabric with country patterns, and gifts. They display candy the old-fashioned way here—in huge glass apothecary jars—while antiques and memorabilia line the overhead shelves.

Teddy bears rule at **Gable House**—hundreds of teddy bears of every possible description. You'll find stuffed bears, wooden-faced bears, and dressed bears (including a wedding party), as well as oak and poplar bear desks, bear chairs, bear clocks, and bear swings.

Gable House also sponsors an Annual Teddy Bear Beauty Pageant and Picnic. Proud bear owners, ages four to ninety-four, show off their bears, which are judged in swimsuit, casual wear, formal wear, and best-dressed couples categories. And best of show honors result in the crowning of Miss Teddy Bear of Grand Rapids, with the winning bear taking home a $25 gift certificate.

Standing in the Grand Battery at **Fort Meigs**, with its three twelve-pounder cannons aimed across the Maumee River, you can almost hear the blast of cannon fire and feel the rain of falling earth and timber from shells exploding nearby. The fort was under siege for nine days and nights in May, 1813, but the American forces in the fort held off the British attack and repelled them again when the British launched a second invasion three months later.

Ohio's role in the War of 1812 is not given much space in the history books, but the American forces, commanded by General William Henry Harrison, twice turned back British offensives at the fort that Harrison named for Ohio's governor at the time, Return Jonathan Meigs. Harrison's forces constructed the fort in early February, 1813, and this fortification became the base for 3,000 troops. On April 28, British forces began to construct a camp and gun batteries opposite Fort Meigs, four batteries across the river and two east of the fort. The British siege began May 1, 1813, and lasted until May 9.

The entire Fort Meigs fortification has been carefully reconstructed, including the seven blockhouses and the 2,000-yard stockade wall. A flat-topped mound of earth built against the inside of the wall forms a banquette (or firing step) where the soldiers stood to fire musket rounds at the invaders attacking the ten-acre fort. Some of the blockhouses today house museums describing the history of the battles here, while others contain twelve-pounder cannons as they did in May, 1813. Signs aid visitors taking a self-guided tour of the fort by explaining the significance of various locations inside the stockade. On weekends, costumed soldiers set up camp at Fort Meigs, further enhancing the sensation that one has stepped back in time to the early nineteenth century. Just outside the stockade walls are picnic tables and barbecue grills.

Fort Meigs is on Rte. 65, west of the intersection with Rte. 25, in Perrysburg; (419) 874-4121. Open Memorial Day to Labor Day, Wednesday through Saturday, 9:30 A.M.–5 P.M.; Sunday, noon–5 P.M. May be open weekends in September and October. Admission: adults, $2; children, (ages six to twelve), $1.

Sandusky County

Rutherford B. Hayes (or "Ruddy" as he was known to his friends) was President of the United States exactly 100 years be-

Fort Meigs

fore Jimmy Carter. For a glimpse at the politics and lifestyle of that era, visit the **Rutherford B. Hayes Presidential Center** in Fremont. The center, on a lush twenty-five acres known as Spiegel Grove, consists of the stately Victorian mansion built for Hayes by his uncle, Sardis Birchard, the expansive Hayes museum, and a presidential library with more than 60,000 volumes.

The museum contains exhibits from Hayes's early career as a lawyer, first in Fremont (which was then known as Lower Sandusky) and later in Cincinnati. Hayes, in fact, was instrumental in having the name of Lower Sandusky changed to Fremont. With nearby towns named Sandusky, Upper Sandusky, and Middle Sandusky, the residents of Fremont gratefully accepted the change, as did the United States Post Office.

It was in Cincinnati that Hayes became involved in politics, and old party tickets indicate his first race was in 1859 for city solicitor. At the outbreak of the Civil War, Hayes enlisted in the Union army, and a letter from his wife, Lucy Webb Hayes, written to him while he was in the army, is on display. Hayes was wounded several times during the war, seriously at the Battle of South Mountain.

Elected to Congress before the war's conclusion, Hayes refused to leave the army to serve his term until the end of the conflict. After his four years in Congress, Hayes was elected governor of Ohio in 1868 and 1870, and again in 1876. The museum's campaign relics include political cartoons, newspaper clippings, hats, and banners. Hayes's favorite chair, which he used while governor, is also there.

Hayes's election to the presidency also took place in 1876, but a dispute over twenty electoral votes was not resolved until March 2, 1877—three days before the inauguration! By an electoral vote count of 185 to 184, Hayes became the nineteenth president of the United States, defeating New York Governor Samuel Tilden. Photographs of the inauguration of Hayes and tickets to inaugural balls are in the museum, as is the Haviland china used by the Hayes White House. A magnificent sideboard carved by Cincinnatian Henry L. Fry for use in the private White House dining room and the presidential glassware used by presidents from Andrew Jackson through Hayes are displayed.

A short walk from the museum across the shady lawn stands the elegant Hayes mansion. This enormous home has thirty to forty rooms (depending on your precise definition of a "room"), and a large front porch faces the towering trees of Spiegel Grove. Members of the Hayes family lived in the mansion until 1966, when it was opened to the public for guided tours.

President and Mrs. Hayes used all the furnishings now in the home when they returned to Fremont from Washington in 1881. Many of the pieces were gifts from around the world which they received when in the White House. While each room has lavish appointments, the dining room, with its massive table for twenty-four guests, is exceptional. Fourteen fireplaces warmed the spacious residence, some with mantels of Italian marble, others of hand-carved hardwoods with tile inserts. The 14-foot ceilings in the drawing room are just tall enough to accommodate the life-size portrait of Hayes and its ornate frame. Throughout the home are the original gas lighting fixtures, which have been converted to electricity.

The Rutherford B. Hayes Presidential Center is at the corner of Buckland and Hayes avenues, in Fremont; (419) 332-2081. Th⌐ museum and residence are open Tuesday through Satur⌐ A.M.–5 P.M.; Sunday, Monday, and holidays, 1:30–5 P.M. ⌐

adults, $2 for museum or residence, $4 for both; children (ages seven–twelve), $1 for museum or residence, $2 for both. The library is open Tuesday through Saturday, 9 A.M.–5 P.M.; no admission charged.

Ottawa County

A half dozen islands are sprinkled in Lake Erie just north of Catawba and Marblehead peninsulas. Easily accessible by air or ferry, **Put-in-Bay** is the center of activity on South Bass Island. A large, protected harbor attracts boaters, who often dock their vessels overnight.

This safe harbor also attracted Commodore Oliver Hazard Perry in 1813. His fleet lay at anchor here before defeating the British fleet commanded by Captain Robert H. Barclay in the Battle of Lake Erie on Sept. 10, 1813. To commemorate Perry's triumph and to pay tribute to the subsequent decades of peaceful relations between the United States and Canada along their lengthy, unfortified border, a monument was constructed at Put-in-Bay. This 352-foot column, built of pink Milford, Massachusetts, granite, has a 45-foot-diameter base. It was built between 1912 and 1915 and is the world's largest Doric column. The Perry Victory and International Peace Memorial's observation deck is open ·to the public daily from late April to late October.

Other Put-in-Bay attractions include shops, restaurants, taverns, and a large, shady park along the marina. The **Blacksmith Shop** on Catawba Avenue has perhaps the most intriguing inventory on the island. Hand-crafted jewelry, unusual baskets, and pottery are attractively displayed, as are the shop's nautical items. These include old brass ships' bells, lights, and even a ship's telegraph.

The Blacksmith Shop is open daily during warmer months from 9:30 A.M. to 6 P.M.; (419) 285-4485.

Phil Gerstner is the inspiration behind the intriguing **Retrospect**, a very different Put-in-Bay shop. Phil works in watercolors, which are available for sale. He also brings together an eclectic collection of other handmade crafts: pottery, unusual wind chimes, custom jewelry (including some very distinctive brass bracelets), and stained glass. Phil's taste ranges from the offbeat to the bizarre (pottery planters shaped like feet!), and his shop is a delight.

First-class nautical memorabilia abound at Robert Stone's and William Timmerman's **Cargo Net**. You can find (and purchase) everything from authentic ships' wheels and massive brass bells to pottery and nautical art in this fabulous shop. Many antique pieces are available—an 1850s-vintage harpoon gun was priced at $6,500 during my last visit here. Also displayed were a spectacular 1870s telescope ($6,200), and a 135-pound ship's bell ($950), plus a World War II diver's suit. For those who hear the call of the sea, a visit to the Cargo Net is a must!

After a walking tour of the town of Put-in-Bay, it's time to explore other points on this small, wooded island. Bicycles are one of the most enjoyable ways to survey South Bass, and rentals are available. Trams, buses, and taxis also transport visitors around the island.

About half way across the island from Put-in-Bay (ten minutes by bicycle) on Catawba Road is **Heineman's Winery and Crystal Cave**. Heineman's offers tours of both a unique geode cave and its winery, as well as selling wine by the glass, bottle, or case. The cave, 40 feet beneath the surface, is actually an unusually large geode. Geodes (stones with a cavity lined with crystal) are relatively common in nature, but they are normally no larger than a baseball or softball. The Crystal Cave geode is large enough to hold thirty people. It was created under pressure over 4.5 million years. The cave remains a cool 52 degrees year-round, and guides explain the history and geology of this unique formation.

After the cave tour, another guide takes you on a tour of the winery. Heineman's grows approximately 40 percent of the grapes they need, purchasing the rest from other island vineyards. From eight different kinds of grapes, Heineman's produces thirteen wines, plus fresh grape juice, with an output of 30,000 gallons of wine and juice annually. The Lake Erie islands are ideally suited for vineyards due to the soil's high limestone content and a relatively late frost because of the warming influence of Lake Erie.

On the winery tour, visitors see large presses which squeeze 180 gallons of juice from each ton of grapes. The grapes ferment in oak barrels, some holding as much as 1,680 gallons, or in stainless steel tanks. Other stops on the winery tour include the bottling, labeling, and packing areas.

After your tour, enjoy a glass of Heineman's wine in the wine garden, which has picnic tables, a fountain, and nicely kept gardens. Cheeseplates are also served.

Heineman's Winery and Crystal Cave tours are given from mid-May through mid-September, 11 A.M.–5 P.M. daily. Admission for both tours is $2 for adults, $1 for children, and it includes a complimentary glass of wine or grape juice. (419) 285-2811.

Across the street from Heineman's is another cave, a much larger one, known as **Perry's Cave**. Commodore Perry is credited with the discovery of this limestone cavern, which measures 208 feet by 165 feet and is 52 feet below the surface. Some evidence suggests that Perry stored ammunition and cannons in the cave prior to the Battle of Lake Erie in 1813, and that British prisoners were held here after Perry's victory.

Along the north wall of the cave is a large pool of crystal-clear water fed by a spring. The luxurious Victory Hotel, once the largest hotel in the world, pumped water from this pool for its drinking water, and the hotel's piping is still visible in the cave. The hotel burned down in 1919, and its ruins are on the south side of the island near South Bass Island State Park.

Perry's Cave is open weekends in May and September, daily during summer months, 11 A.M.–6 P.M.; (419) 285-2405. Admission: adults, $1.50; children (ages six to twelve), 75¢.

Traveling to South Bass Island is relatively easy most of the year, with Parker Boat Line, (419) 285-3491 or (419) 732-2800, offering ferry service from Port Clinton to Put-in-Bay, and Miller Boat Line, (419) 285-2421, providing ferry service from the Catawba peninsula to the south end of the island. Both companies ferry both autos and passengers, though reservations are sometimes required for automobiles. Ferry service to the island is available only from mid-April through mid-November, because the island is iced-in during winter months.

While some brave (or perhaps foolhardy) travelers drive across the ice to the island in winter, year-round air service is provided by Island Airlines, which bills itself as the "shortest airline in the world." Island Airlines is based at Port Clinton's airport, 3255 East State Road, (419) 734-3149, (419) 285-3371.

The **Island House** in downtown Port Clinton proves that the good life can continue well beyond 100 years. This restored jewel of a hotel was built in 1886 and has been the focal point of this Lake Erie community for years. But by the early 1980s it had fallen into disrepair (I visited it while working on the first edition of this book and did not include the place because of its deteriorating condition).

But James V. Stouffer, Jr., and Associates breathed new life into this magnificent old hotel, purchasing it in 1986 and promptly spending more than $2 million renovating it. This top-to-bottom restoration has been very successful—the result is a thoroughly modern hotel with the ambiance of a turn-of-the-century inn. Today, the Island House has plenty of what real estate agents refer to as "curb appeal." It's a substantial three-story brick structure, trimmed in pure white, with outdoor awnings and pleasing landscaping.

Inside, the thirty-seven guest rooms are tastefully decorated and modern. Classy carpeting and wallcoverings, often in stylish grays and mauves, can be found throughout the hotel. A massive oak bar, plenty of natural woodwork, and the original stamped metal ceiling make the Island House tavern a delight.

Chef John Wrobbel, formerly of the Detroit Athletic Club, presides over the kitchen that serves the Victory Dining Room, where fresh Lake Erie perch and pickerel dishes number more than a half dozen. But the menu doesn't end with local fish—steaks, veal, chicken, pork, frog legs, lobster tails, and much more also await hungry travelers.

Latest additions to the Island House are the new executive suites, which cater to corporate charter fishing groups. And the Madison Street Cafe now offers casual dining in a light and informal atmosphere.

The Island House is located at 102 Madison Street, Port Clinton; (800) 233-7307 (Ohio toll-free), (419) 734-2166. Rates: $30 to $75 per night for two people, depending on room and season. Visa, MasterCard, and American Express are accepted. Open year-round.

The Lake Erie islands and nearby coastal towns were once the center of champagne production in the United States, and that tradition continues at the historic **Mon Ami Winery**, which also houses a pleasant restaurant. This winery has been in continuous operation since 1870, producing champagne by the old-fashioned "method champenoise," the French technique of fermenting in the bottle.

Constructed of native stone and walnut, the restaurant and winery are surrounded by tall trees and lovely gardens. Old aging barrels are stacked behind the building and are available for sale. Reds and oranges are the dominant colors in the spacious main dining room, with its beamed ceiling, circular booths, and fancy wine bar at the far end of the room.

The dinner menu at Mon Ami presents delights such as Long Island duckling a l'orange, barbecued baby back ribs, deep-fried chicken, and a choice of steaks. For seafood lovers, a half dozen entrees are offered, including whole lake pickerel, broiled scampi with shallot and garlic butter sauce, and deep-fried Lake Erie perch. After your dinner, the dessert cart will tempt you with sweets: cheesecake topped with chocolate, amaretto pie, and fresh fruit, to name a few. For lunch at Mon Ami, your choices include homemade soups, fresh salads, a number of sandwiches, and entrees such as turkey divan, eggplant Parmesan, and breaded scallops.

Mon Ami's complete selection of wines and champagnes, made from Lake Erie islands grapes, are available with your meal, and a large wine store sells bottles and cases of these wines, as well as the popular champagne celery seed salad dressing. Tours of the winery are given daily at 2 P.M. and 4 P.M. (times may change, so call ahead).

Mon Ami Restaurant and Winery is on Catawba Island (which used to be an island, but is now a peninsula) at 3845 East Wine Cellar Road, just off Rte. 53, east of Port Clinton; (419) 797-4445. Open for lunch Monday through Saturday, 11:30 A.M.–4 P.M., and for dinner Monday through Saturday, 4–10 P.M. Sunday dinner is noon–9 P.M. Prices: lunch, inexpensive to moderate; dinner, moderate to expensive. MasterCard, Visa, and American Express are accepted.

For those seeking fine Catawba Island dining in a more contemporary setting, I recommend the pleasing **Greenhouse Restaurant**. Overlooking a well-manicured golf course and lush patio, this delightful place offers a light and airy ambiance created by skylights, ceiling fans, huge expanses of glass, hanging plants, and plenty of white. Accent walls of exposed brick and classy table settings finish off the tasteful decor at the Greenhouse. Many of the restaurant's windows face west, so every sunset here is a special occasion.

More than a dozen seafood dishes tempt diners at the Greenhouse—everything from fresh Lake Erie perch and pickerel to seafood fettucine. Salmon marinara and Manhattan scallops are favorites, as is the seafood brochette—sea scallops and jumbo shrimp broiled with choice veggies and served on a bed of rice.

Meat-eaters won't be disappointed either; the Greenhouse presents specialties such as its own version of veal oscar (sauteed veal topped with steamed asparagus and shrimp and laced with bearnaise sauce). Fancy poultry and a selection of steaks round out the menu. And combinations of sirloin or prime rib and Alaskan king crab or lobster tail are often available.

For more casual food and spirits, stop in next door at the adjoining Side Door tavern. It's a friendly, peanut-shells-on-the-floor kind of place that serves as a neighborhood bar.

The Greenhouse Restaurant is at 3026 Northwest Catawba Road on Catawba Island; (419) 797-4411. Open for lunch and dinner every day in the summer; open Tuesday through Sunday in September, October, and May; Thursday through Sunday in December, March, and April; closed in January and February. Prices: moderate to expensive; Visa, MasterCard, and American Express are accepted.

Not far away is one of the most popular public beaches on Lake Erie—the lengthy stretch of sand at **East Harbor State Park**. Lifeguards watch swimmers during summer months, and there are snack bars and bathhouses (with showers). Unfortunately, a fierce storm in 1972 severely damaged the original beach area, and it is no longer open to swimmers.

In addition to the lakefront beach, the park contains 800 acres of water in three protected harbors. Middle Harbor, with its restriction on motorboats, offers an ideal environment for the thousands of resident and migratory waterfowl attracted to the lush acreage, making bird watching a favorite pastime. East Harbor State Park is the home of many black-crowned night herons, and a large great blue heron nesting ground is nearby.

Boat launching ramps are in the park, and a park naturalist conducts nature programs during the summer. Winter sports at East Harbor include ice fishing, ice boating, skating, sledding, and snowmobiling.

East Harbor State Park is on Buck Road off Rte. 269, near the junction of Rtes. 269 and 163, Marblehead; (419) 734-4424.

The 100-room **Hotel Lakeside**, a large Victorian structure painted white with black trim, faces Lake Erie on a shady lot at the water's edge. This three-story frame hotel was built in 1875, with additions completed in 1879 and 1890. The hotel is part of the community of Lakeside, a one-square-mile educational, cultural, recreational, and religious center listed on the National Register of Historic Places. Lakeside consists of hotels, cottages, private homes, shops, restaurants, and recreation facilities, which are used by both guests and residents of this unique village. A modest gate fee is levied during summer months, and with payment of that fee, visitors may use the tennis courts, playgrounds, and volleyball and basketball courts, and may swim and fish off the community's pier. A nightly program of lectures, theater, concerts, and movies is offered in Hoover Auditorium during the summer.

At the Hotel Lakeside, a large yet homey structure, guests can enjoy the evening paper on the long, screened porch or on the lawn furniture between the hotel and Lake Erie. The spacious lobby is furnished with wicker chairs and couches and a variety of antiques. The guest rooms are gradually being restored with period wallpapers and furnishings such as marble-topped washstands. All have the high ceilings of the era, and many come equipped with ceiling fans. The first-floor dining room serves three meals daily and offers a pleasant view of the lake.

From the pier, visitors and residents of Lakeside enjoy the colorful sunsets, and sailing lessons are available. The shuffleboard and miniature golf areas attract crowds on warm summer evenings in this family-oriented community. Lakeside may not be everyone's ideal vacation or getaway choice—those looking for chic nightclubs will surely be disappointed. But for those who seek a serene and peaceful place to enjoy Lake Erie, Lakeside may be the perfect destination.

The Hotel Lakeside is north of Rte. 163 on North Shore Boulevard in Lakeside; (419) 798-4461. Since the hotel is not heated (nor air-conditioned, for that matter), its season runs only from the first of June through Labor Day. Rates: $20 to $40 per night; the less expensive rooms are not yet restored and share a community bath. MasterCard and Visa are accepted.

For charming Lakeside accommodations on a smaller scale, try the century-old **Poor Richards Inn**. Innkeeper Jeanne Christopher provides bed-and-breakfast–style hospitality in a cheerful cozy inn. Its 1920s decor creates a homey atmosphere, and white wicker rockers await you on the porch. Most guest rooms share a bath down the hall, which seems appropriate at this type of establishment. Guests freely roam the kitchen and dining room, as well as Jeanne's antique shop.

Poor Richards Inn is located at 317 Maple Avenue, Lakeside; (419) 798-5405 (summer); (614) 861-8780 (rest of the year). Poor Richards Inn is open daily in summer and on spring and fall

Marblehead Lighthouse

weekends. Rates: $18–$37 per day, including continental breakfast; weekly rates are also available. Personal checks are accepted. (Lakeside lodging is available year-round at the community's Fountain Inn.)

Standing guard at what is known as the "roughest point in Lake Erie," the **Marblehead Lighthouse** is the oldest continuously operating lighthouse on the Great Lakes. The shallow water in this part of the lake, along with the 200 miles of open water between Buffalo and Marblehead, allow howling northeasters to generate waves 10 to 15 feet tall. The crash of those waves against the rocks around the lighthouse often shoots spray all the way up to the beacon 67 feet above the water. The Marblehead Lighthouse, built of native limestone in 1821, originally used candles for its light. Oil-burning lamps replaced the candles and were later themselves replaced by an electric light and a 300-millimeter glass lens, which make the beacon visible for 7 miles.

While rough water often bashes this peninsula in the spring and fall, peaceful days prevail in the summer. Picnic tables near the lighthouse make this an excellent place to stop and relax as you explore the Lake Erie shoreline.

The Marblehead Lighthouse is off Rte. 163 in Marblehead. Open daylight hours; no admission charge.

Erie County

Four miles north of Marblehead and 9 miles northwest of Sandusky is Kelleys Island. It was originally called Cunningham Island, named for the island's first white inhabitant, who lived here from 1800 to 1812. But Indians visited the island sometime between A.D. 1200 and 1600 and created the inscriptions (or pictographs) pecked into the 32-by-21-foot flat-topped slab of limestone known as **Inscription Rock**. The rock rests on the water's edge on the south side of the island, and its pictographs have nearly been erased by erosion. Fortunately, a visitor here in 1850, U.S. Army Captain Seth Eastman, made a permanent record of the inscriptions. He carefully measured and drew in detail the pictographs, and from his drawings, reliefs have been made of these inscriptions. These reliefs, including the one exhibited at Inscription Rock, clearly reveal at least eight human figures wearing headdresses etched in the rock, plus bird and animal figures.

Inscription Rock is near the intersection of Water Street and

Addison Road on the south side of Kelleys Island. Open daylight hours; no admission charge.

The quarries on 2,800-acre Kelleys Island once dug and loaded 500 1,000-ton boatloads of limestone annually, and vineyards, wineries, and fruit and vegetable farms flourished. At the turn of the century, the island had a year-round population of 1,700. Today, the quarries have closed and farming activity has declined, but the island, with a year-round population of approximatly 100, offers restaurants, lodging, bicycle and boat rentals, and tram tours to visitors.

One of the more intriguing lodgings is across the street from Inscription Rock—the **Kelley Mansion**. Datus Kelley built this three-story gray stone home as a wedding gift for his son Addison in the early 1860s. Datus and his brother Irad, both from the Cleveland area, first visited the island in 1833, and they eventually purchased every acre of it at prices ranging from $1.50 to $5 per acre.

Over the years, the mansion has had a number of owners who used it for a variety of purposes, including forty years as a Dominican camp. The Lemley family, William and Garnet and their son Bill, purchased the mansion in 1979 and now rent rooms in this unique structure.

Gray fieldstones form the exterior walls, which are trimmed in ornate white filigree, and a cupola perches on the rooftop. Tall trees shade the lot, and a knight in armor stands on the front porch, presumably greeting visitors. Across the street is a private sand beach for the mansion's guests.

As you step through the front door, you immediately notice the oak and cherry spiral staircase in the center hall. It was built without a single nail, and it seems remarkable that this floating staircase stands, much less that it can actually support any weight. Red Italian glass fills the skylight directly above the stairs.

Other original features of the home include the tulip and oak hardwood floors and the Italian marble fireplaces. The Kelley family coat of arms still hangs over the fireplace in the front parlor; guests use this room for reading and relaxing. The mansion has 12-foot ceilings, and the massive 200-pound doors are solid wood and perfectly balanced. Many of the first floor rooms still have the original shutters, which cleverly fold into a recess in the walls when not in use. The bedrooms are simply but adequately furnished, and guests share a community bath.

The Kelley Mansion is at the corner of Lakeshore and Addison

Road, Kelleys Island; (419) 746-2273, (304) 525-1919. Open May through September. Rates: $30 to $70 per night. Reservations are recommended.

It's pleasant fifteen-minute bicycle ride to the north side of the island—the site of the **Glacial Grooves**. A glacier moving down from Labrador, Canada, scoured these grooves into the limestone bedrock. The grooved limestone is a trough 400 feet long, 25 to 35 feet wide, and 10 to 15 feet deep, and it's one of the most accessible examples of such grooves in the world.

These grooves were formed at a time when this part of the earth was much colder and wetter than today. Snow and ice would not completely melt during the short summers 30,000 years ago, so an ever deeper mass of frozen snow accumulated. As the weight of this mass increased, the glacier crept southward at the rate of an inch or two per day, taking 5,000 years to arrive at the site of the Glacial Grooves. The pressure of that mass, which was up to a mile deep, carved the grooves still visible in the island's limestone. Even more spectacular grooves once existed in this area, but they were destroyed by a nearby quarrying operation.

The Glacial Grooves are at the north end of Division Street, Kelleys Island. Open daylight hours, no admission charge.

Just across the road from the Glacial Grooves is **Kelleys Island State Park**. The park offers campsites (rented on first-come, first-serve basis), a sandy swimming beach, and boat ramps; (419) 746-2546.

The Neuman Boat Line provides daily ferry service between Kelleys Island and Marblehead from April through November, and in July and August service is also provided Monday through Saturday from Sandusky; (419) 626-5557, 746-2261. The Griffing Flying Service provides air transport to the island from the Griffing-Sandusky Airport; (419) 626-5161. Island Airlines, (419) 734-3149, flies between Kelleys Island and the Port Clinton airport.

Back on the mainland, amusement park aficionados will definitely want to visit one of Ohio's most popular such parks, **Cedar Point**. Situated at the tip of a long, narrow peninsula jutting out into Lake Erie, this 364-acre park delights guests with a wide assortment of rides (including seven coasters), more than 100 entertainers performing in live shows, dolphin and sea lion demonstrations, and wild animal acts. For those needing accommodations at Cedar Point, the park has its own 400-room Victorian

151

hotel with a private beach on Lake Erie. The Hotel Breakers was built in 1905 and has rooms and suites ranging in price from $55 to $110 per night. The hotel is open from late May to early September. Cedar Point also has a large marina on the lake, with slips available for day rental.

Cedar Point is on the Cedar Point Causeway, north of Sandusky; (419) 626-0830. Open from mid-May through mid-September.

After a day at Cedar Point or the Lake Erie islands, nothing sounds better than a fresh seafood dinner. One of the best seafood restaurants along the lake is in the harbor town of Huron— the **Twine House**. The original structure on this site was built in the 1840s. In 1859, the roof was raised when the building was converted to a maintenance shop for wood-burning locomotives, and the splices made in the support columns to raise the roof are still visible today. In later years, both ships and wooden fishing boxes were assembled here. This building's last incarnation prior to becoming a restaurant was as a storage shed for commercial fishing nets, or "twine"—hence the name, the Twine House.

The interior of the Twine House has exposed beams and brick, and a wall of windows look out on the Huron River. Both commercial and pleasure craft ply the Huron heading toward or returning from Lake Erie. For those traveling the river, the Twine House offers diners its private dock.

The dilemma faced by seafood lovers at this restaurant is choosing from the wide variety of dishes: lobster tails, baked stuffed flounder, fried Lake Erie perch and pickerel, broiled halibut, Alaskan king crab, and many others. Other dinner entrees include steaks, broiled pork chops, fried chicken, and ham steak Hawaiian. While they mull over the menu, customers are served two complimentary appetizers: a delicious cheese spread with garlic toast or crackers and a seasoned mushroom dip with fresh vegetables.

Lunch at the Twine House is more casual, with a large selection of sandwiches (including a fresh perch sandwich) and plates such as open-face steak, chopped sirloin, liver and onions, and a choice of omelets. Homemade pies are available with lunch or dinner, and every Sunday the Twine House prepares a lavish buffet.

The Twine House is at 132 North Main Street, Huron; (419) 433-2035. Open for lunch Monday through Friday, 11 A.M.–3 P.M.; Saturday, 11 A.M.–3:30 P.M.; for dinner Monday through Thursday,

5–11 P.M.; until midnight on Friday and Saturday; Sunday, 11 A.M.–10 P.M. Prices: lunch, inexpensive; dinner, moderate to expensive. MasterCard and Visa are accepted.

After your meal, take a walking tour of the boardwalk along the Huron River. Many fine pleasure craft dock in the boat basin, and commercial vessels can be seen at the ore and grain docks.

Not far from the river is the **Wileswood Country Store**, an enjoyable place to browse because of its unusual inventory. Stocked with many items one would find in an old-fashioned general store, Wileswood's merchandise includes fabric, books, wooden toys, Christmas ornaments, and glassware. They stock their own brand of applebutter, honey, and preserves, and fresh popcorn is prepared frequently. Other offerings include leather goods, bells of all types, kazoos, bosun's pipes, ink wells, and quill pens. A fancy candy counter tempts people of all ages, and there is a wide selection of teas, herbs, and spices.

The Wileswood Country Store is on Rtes. 2 and 6, just west of the bridge crossing the Huron River, Huron; (419) 433-4244. Open Monday through Saturday, 9 A.M.–5:30 P.M.; Sunday, noon–5:30 P.M.; open daily until 9 P.M. in summer.

The achievements of Ohio-born Thomas Edison are staggering—he invented the phonograph, the incandescent light, the motion picture camera, the fluoroscope, the nickel-iron-alkaline battery. In fact, at the time of his death Edison held 1,093 different American patents.

The Edison Museum and Birthplace in Milan provides an opportunity for visitors to learn more about this prolific inventor. Edison's father, Samuel, was involved in the Papineau-Mackenzie Rebellion, an unsuccessful Canadian counterpart to the American Revolution. Samuel and his wife, Nancy, migrated to Milan in 1839, attracted by the boom in shipping created there by the canal linking Milan, an inland community, with Lake Erie. In fact, in the 1840s, Milan was one of the world's major grain ports and shipbuilding centers. For example, in 1847, 918,000 bushels of grain were shipped from Milan, and fourteen warehouses loaded as many as twenty schooners per day—amazing statistics for a town 7 miles from the lakefront! Milan's boom was short-lived, however, for the coming of the railroad and the flood of 1868 ended the town's brief era as a port.

The small, red brick house where Edison was born on Feb. 11, 1847, is just up the hill from the former location of Milan's warehouses and port. The Edison home and adjacent small museum contain a number of his inventions—an early mimeograph machine (which Edison sold to the A.B. Dick Company in 1887), phonographs, telegraph equipment, dictating machines, motion picture cameras—and a model of Edison's 1893 movie studio, called the "Black Maria," which rotated and had an adjustable opening in the roof to allow sunlight to illuminate the stages.

Pictures of Edison with family and friends like Henry Ford adorn the walls of the home, and Edison's hat, cape, cane, and slippers are displayed, as is an unusual pig-shaped footstool. Edison bought his birthplace from his sister in 1906 and was shocked to find on a visit here in 1923 that this house did not yet have electric lights, a situation he quickly remedied.

The Edison Museum and Birthplace is north of Rte. 113 at 9 North Edison Drive, Milan; (419) 499-2135. Open February through November, Tuesday through Sunday, 1–5 P.M. (last tour at 4:30); opens at 10 A.M. Tuesday through Saturday in the summer. Admission: adults, $2; children (ages six to fourteen), $1.

Two blocks from Edison's birthplace is Milan's central business district, which was built around a one-square-block park. One-hundred-year-old buildings house many of the town's shops, and these restored buildings and the shady park make Milan a pleasant stop. In addition to antique and gift shops, the square has a restaurant, the **Milan Inn**, which offers tasty lunches and dinners to travelers and townspeople alike. Inside this former stagecoach stop, built in 1845, murals depict Milan's roller-coaster prosperity, including the boom of the great canal era.

Immediately after you're seated, a tray of warm rolls and bread will be brought to your table. The tempting "sticky rolls" truly melt in your mouth, and the waitress will stop by frequently, giving you ample opportunity to eat too many before your meal.

For lunch, select from entrees such as roast leg of lamb, barbecue spareribs, broiled pork chops, and fried lake perch. The dinner menu features a choice of steaks, chops, prime rib, and nearly a dozen seafood dishes, including broiled monkfish and a broiled seafood platter.

The Milan Inn is at 29 East Church Street, Milan; (419) 499-4604. Open Tuesday through Friday, 11 A.M.–9 P.M.; Saturday and Sunday, 8 A.M.–8 P.M. Prices: lunch, inexpensive to moderate; dinner, moderate to expensive. MasterCard, Visa, and American Express are accepted.

Vermilion is perhaps Ohio's most picturesque Lake Erie coastal town, with quaint homes set on meandering lagoons, sumptuous sail and power pleasure craft, and fine dining. Vermilion exudes a peaceful and prosperous existence—one of sun, seafood, and recreation.

McGarvey's Riverview Restaurant, located on the Vermilion River not far from the spot where the river spills into Lake Erie, has served outstanding seafood for more than forty years. In the summer, many families arrive by boat and use the private docks. In the spacious bar, standing rigging disappears into the peaked, high ceiling, and blocks and tackle, ships' lanterns, and wheels give the lounge the appearance of the foredeck on an old schooner.

The west wall of the three large dining rooms is glass, so diners watch the busy recreational boat traffic on the river. These three rooms seat 550 customers. The dinner menu offers seafood in every conceivable form and fashion—from the very popular New England clam chowder to the steamed cherrystone clams. Dinner entrees include broiled lobster tails, fried deep sea scallops, and the fresh catch of the day. A half dozen cuts of steak are offered, as are steak and seafood combinations such as the scampi 'n' steak. Wednesday night during summer months, McGarvey's offers its sip, sup, and sail dinners, which include a cocktail, a choice of four dinners, and a moonlight cruise on Lake Erie aboard McGarvey's own party boat.

McGarvey's Riverview Restaurant is at 5150 Liberty Avenue (Rte. 6), in Vermilion; (216) 967-8771. Open Tuesday through Sunday, 1:30–10 P.M. (plus Mondays during the summer). Open weekends only in January and February. Prices: lunch, moderate; dinner, expensive. MasterCard, Visa, and American Express are accepted.

One other Vermilion restaurant warrants special attention—Zdenka and Karel Vetrovsky's **Old Prague Restaurant**. Set in a delightful cedar structure in the center of Vermilion's shopping district, this distinctive establishment serves both Old World recipes and American favorites. The large, open dining area offers a homey, comfortable setting, and the friendly people at Old Prague make guests feel almost like family.

The specialties at Old Prague are the "Nationality Favorites," which include Hungarian goulash and chicken paprikash (farm-fresh chicken in a zesty sour cream sauce). Two other popular entrees are roast duck and roast pork, which are served with sauerkraut. All meals come with traditional egg dumplings.

American dinner entrees include Boston strip and porterhouse steaks, grilled lamb chops, and honey-dipped chicken. Those who favor fish can choose from a half dozen dinners such as fresh Lake Erie perch and a fisherman's platter. Lunch selections include salads, sandwiches, and entrees—roast chicken with stuffing for example. Two homemade soups are served daily.

The Old Prague Restaurant is at 5586 Liberty Avenue (Rte. 6), Vermilion; (216) 967-7182. Open Monday, Tuesday, and Thursday, noon–7:30 P.M.; Friday and Saturday, noon–8 P.M.; Sunday from noon–7 P.M. Summer hours slightly later; closed in February. Prices: inexpensive to moderate. MasterCard and Visa are accepted.

Across the street from Old Prague Restaurant is an intriguing shop—the **Musik Box Haus**. Owner Genevieve Smith Clark has collected handcrafted music boxes from all over the world—Steinbachs from Germany, Sorrentos from Italy, and music box movements including Swiss-made Thorens and Reuge. The hundreds of music boxes in stock are constructed of fine woods, metals, and fabrics, in every size and shape conceivable.

Also on display is a true masterpiece—the large Porter Music Box. The mahogany case, inlaid with black ebony, white holly, tulip wood, and burl, is finished with five coats of hand-rubbed lacquer. Constructed in New England, the Porter plays two seventy-eight-note copper discs.

The Musik Box Haus is at 5551 Liberty Avenue (Rte. 6), Vermilion; (216) 967-4744. Summer hours: Monday through Thursday, 9 A.M.–6 P.M.; Friday and Saturday, 9 A.M.–9 P.M.; Sunday, noon–5 P.M. Winter hours: Monday through Saturday, 10 A.M.–6 P.M.; Sunday, noon–5 P.M.

The **Great Lakes Museum**, appropriately located on the Lake Erie shore in picturesque Vermilion, has two floors of marine exhibits, photos, and paintings dedicated to the history and lore of the Great Lakes. Navigation equipment, such as ships' telegraphs, compasses, barographs, and a pelorus (bearing finder) are displayed, as are ships' bells, fog horns, and a collection of old nameboards from Great Lakes schooners, freighters, and steamers. The museum also contains the figurehead (or busthead) from an unidentified schooner, c. 1855, which was part of the Cheseborough Lumber Company fleet.

Dozens of old life rings are scattered throughout the museum, including one from the ill-fated *Edmund Fitzgerald*, which went down in Lake Superior on Nov. 10, 1975. The lower level houses a prize-winning wooden 18-foot double ender, built in 1937, and the complete steam engine from the tug *Roger*, built in 1913. The museum has also acquired several artifacts from the 1813 Battle of Lake Erie, including some old timbers from Commodore Perry's flagship, *Niagara*, plus a grapnel and spike from that vessel, and the telescope used by Perry's staff during the battle.

The Great Lakes Museum is at 480 Main Street, Vermilion; (216) 967-3467. Open daily from 10 A.M.–5 P.M. (weekends only in winter months). Admission: adults, $2; children (under age sixteen), 75¢.

Huron County

The Firelands region of Ohio takes its name from the Revolutionary War period. While the British held New York City, they made frequent raids against the coastal towns in Connecticut, burning homes, barns, and stores. After the conflict, the citizens petitioned the new state of Connecticut for compensation for their losses, and, in 1792, the "fire-sufferers" were awarded land on the western edge of Connecticut's Western Reserve lands in Ohio—the Firelands.

The **Firelands Museum** is operated by the Firelands Historical Society, the second oldest such society in the state. The museum was described by the society's first members as merely a "cabinet of curios," but today hundreds of items are on display in the two-story Preston-Wickham house, which local newspaper editor Samuel Preston built in 1835 as a wedding present for his daughter, Lucy, and her husband, Frederick Wickham. The extensive gun collection includes dozens of weapons: pistols, rifles, and muskets, some made before the American Revolution, plus military swords and knives. In the Indian exhibit are moccasins, beads, baskets, and tomahawks, as well as ancient points, gouges, and hatchets.

The basement is filled with an impressive group of pioneer tools, such as a 6-foot blacksmith's bellows, a yarn winder and spinning wheel, butter churns, farm implements, and game traps. On the second floor is a marvelous wooden Indian (c. 1860) that once stood in front of a local tobacco shop and the bell clapper from the old Norwalk courthouse that burned down in 1913 (the bell melted in the heat). Period clothing and personal items from early residents of the region are exhibited, as is the first organ manufactured by Norwalk's A.B. Chase Company in the 1870s.

The Firelands Museum is at 4 Case Avenue, Norwalk; (419) 668-6038. Open daily in July and August, 9 A.M.–6 P.M.; Sundays, noon–6 P.M. In May, June, September, and October, the museum is open Tuesday through Sunday, noon–6 P.M. The Firelands Museum is open weekends only in April and November, noon–6 P.M., and is closed December through March. Admission: adults, $1; children (ages twelve to eighteen), 50¢.

When John Wright arrived in America in 1843, a young man of twenty, he dreamed of one day building a vast estate similar to those in his native England. Forty years later, after acquiring 2,400 acres, he established a sawmill and kiln to prepare lumber and brick for what is today known as Wright Mansion.

When listed on the National Register of Historic Places in 1974, the Wright family home was declared significant as "an unusually substantial and stately example of the Second Empire–style mansion found as a relatively isolated farmhouse rather than an urban residence." But for a "farmhouse," Wright's home was constructed with many surprisingly modern conveniences, thanks to his ingenuity. For example, he installed two bathrooms with running water and flush toilets, supplied with water pumped by a windmill to a large tank on the third floor. This at a time— the 1880s—when most rural residences still used water pitchers and chamber pots.

Piped natural gas was unheard of in this country setting before 1900, but Wright developed his own gas system, making acetylene in a small brick building at a corner of his front yard and routing it to chandeliers on all three floors of his home. And a central heating plant in the basement sent hot water to radiators throughout the house.

The Wright Mansion is the centerpiece of **Historic Lyme Village**, a nine-structure collection of historic buildings brought together a decade ago. Tours of Wright Mansion take visitors past magnificent woodwork used throughout this expansive residence: beams and rafters of oak; walnut, curly maple, and cherry for the intricate interior trim. After walking past the huge parlor doors, visitors find room after room of period furnishings, including two of Wright's pianos. A graceful staircase ascends to the second floor, which has eight bedrooms. Most of the third floor is a huge ballroom, with a stage set directly under the central tower at the front of the home.

More rustic structures make up the rest of Lyme Village. Ohio settler pieces, such as a rope bed, spinning wheel, and wood

Historic Lyme Village

cooking stove furnish Annie Brown's log home, built in 1851 in Seneca County. Ms. Brown occupied this modest cabin from 1869 until 1951.

Spinning and weaving exhibits (and occasional demonstrations) can be found in the Schriner-Weidinger Log House, an 1870-vintage structure that was used as a residence until 1947. Other occasional Lyme Village demonstrations include blacksmithing and woodworking at the North Adams Barn, built more than a century ago.

Antique farm implements fill the Biebricher Centennial Barn (erected in 1876), a gothic board-and-batten building with unusual louvred windows. The Seymour House, moved to Lyme Village in 1976 to save it from demolition, is one of the oldest homes in this part of Ohio, and it served as the Seymour family home for more than a century (1836–1948). It likely was a stop on the Underground Railroad. Today it houses country furnishings typical of the early nineteenth century, including a fabulous old pump organ.

Lyme Village also includes a unique museum—the Postmark Collectors Club Museum. Formerly housed in private homes and even a converted school bus at one point, the museum has found a permanent home in a building that twice served as the Lyme, Ohio, post office. Millions of postmarks—the "cancels" used by postal authorities to show where mail originated and to void stamps—fill the museum, the most extensive such collection in the world.

Historic Lyme Village is just east of Bellevue on Rte. 113; (419) 483-4949. Tours are given daily except Monday, June through August, 1–5 P.M. Open weekends only in May and September. Admission: adults, $4; students, $2.50; children under age twelve free.

Railroad buffs, youngsters and anyone who has ever dreamed of being the engineer on a fast-moving freight as it streaks across the countryside will want to climb aboard the many trains displayed at the **Mad River & NKP Railroad Society Museum**. On self-guided tours of the rail yard, you'll discover a number of intriguing locomotives, passenger cars, and even cabooses. Many of these are open, permitting you literally to walk through railroad history.

Those who are knowledgable about trains especially appreciate some of the new Nickel Plate Road additions to the museum's collection, including an Alco RSD-12 Diesel and Dynamometer Car X50041. But anyone will enjoy visiting the RPO Post Office Car, complete with mail sacks, sorting bins, and mail crane. Inside the Nickel Plate Box Car and Fruit Growers Refrigerator Car are extensive displays of railroad models, lanterns, locks, timetables, signs, photos, badges, and the like.

And when you climb in the cab of the museum's Wabash F Diesel, you can't help but imagine yourself racing along the main line from New York to Chicago, or crossing the Rockies on your way to deliver freight to the West Coast. From the cupola of a caboose, you get a feel for the working environment at the other end of a long freight, while tours of America's first dome car demonstrate how trains treated their passengers in days gone by.

An old section house serves as the gift shop and office for the museum. It's staffed by volunteers, many of them current and former railroad workers who enjoy answering your questions and explaining the almost religious attraction of a life on the rails.

The Mad River & NKP Railroad Society Museum is at 253 South West Street, Bellevue, (419) 483-2222. Open Tuesday through Sunday, 1–5 P.M., Memorial Day to Labor Day; weekends only in May and September; Sundays only in October. No admission charge, but donations are appreciated.

Index

Index

Index